Chu~~ck Smith~~

A MEMOIR OF GRACE

AS TOLD TO
Chuck Smith, jr.

THE WORD
FOR TODAY

P.O. Box 8000, Costa Mesa, CA 92628 • Web site: www.twft.com • E-mail: info@twft.com

CHUCK SMITH
A Memoir of Grace

As Told to Chuck Smith, jr.
Edited by Shannon Woodward

Published by The Word For Today
P.O. Box 8000, Costa Mesa, CA 92628
Web site: http://www.twft.com
(800) 272-WORD (9673)

© 2009 The Word For Today
ISBN: 978-1-59751-093-6

Printed in the United States of America.

CONTENTS

FOREWORD

APART FROM CONSIDERABLE URGING, I doubt that Dad would have ever written his autobiography. He loves to talk about God and is convinced that all of the important stories are found in Him. Regarding himself, however, Dad is always surprised that anyone would want to learn about his background, childhood, or personal history.

That being said, Dad has told many stories of his growing-up years in Bible studies when illustrating the meaning of a passage or the power of God's grace. Even those vignettes reveal the richness of a life that was filled with the knowledge of God and guided by the devotion of a loving mother from an early age.

Although my father would not have bothered to sit down and write an autobiography, I felt his story would be extremely helpful to young ministers and inspiring to growing Christians. If they could see Dad's journey in perspective—the successes and the failures, the joys and the sorrows, the high places where God had placed his feet, and the valley of death's dark shadow through which God led him—they might gain a new appreciation for their own struggles, and for the fact that "we must through much tribulation enter into the kingdom of God" (Acts 14:22).

Because Dad makes ministry look easy, it is possible for a young person to think all that is needed to be a pastor is to get in front of people, open a Bible, and start talking. Dad's story, however, reveals the years of fire and flood, persistence and hard work that went into the person he has become and the ministry to which he has been called. It reveals a man committed to personal integrity and financial stewardship (a banker once told him, "You are the only one who has beaten us at our own business"); a man determined to develop his leadership and communication skills.

The day I met with my father to begin working on this project, I set my tape recorder on his desk, turned it on, and held my pen over a notepad as an eager scribe. But first I posed a challenge. "Dad," I began, "you are going to be telling your life's story, so we will cover various events in your childhood, youth, and so on. But we need to be thinking about a *theme*."

Dad nodded in agreement as though he fully understood.

Still, I felt it necessary to clearly explain what I had in mind. "Your life is not only a series of stories, it is also a message. We need to find that central theme that defines those stories and holds them all together."

I had barely finished the sentence when Dad said with obvious conviction, "God prepares His vessel."

Dad's answer came instantly, as though he had been thinking about the meaning of his life's journey for some time. It is typical of him that he would refer to himself in the third person and with a biblical quotation (Romans 9:20-23; 2 Timothy 2:20-21). The moment he spoke those words, my mind went to all the hard years, the various small churches, the hours he logged directing summer camps for poor kids, and the extra jobs he took on just to get by.

I was silent, musing on the fact that my father obviously sees himself as defined by God's will. He then added, "Everything is preparation for something else."

What a wonderful perspective to have on one's life. No single event, regardless of how wonderful or tragic, explains itself. Instead, as believers, we have to be able to see the place each event occupies in the big picture of God's plan. Otherwise, we will not be able to discern the significance of all the things that happen to us while passing through life. There are only two ways we are able to see how various events fit into God's overall scheme: First, in retrospect as we look back and see how all things have worked for good, and secondly, by faith.

The message of my father's autobiography, therefore, is that seasons of preparation have been followed by seasons of service, and seasons of planting seeds have been followed by seasons of harvest. Still today, the good and the bad that enter Dad's daily life are tools in God's hands, preparing him for something else. Only now it is much easier for him to rest in that knowledge than when he was a young man first starting out in ministry.

The book you are reading is my father's story, told in his own words. I have merely served as his scribe. But I have to say that the hours we spent together revisiting his early life have been thoroughly enjoyable for me. I have also cherished the many phone calls we shared as I sought details or clarification regarding specific people, places, dates, or episodes. I learned a few things about Dad that I had not known, and I was especially moved by his candor when he described his dismal failure that caused him to walk away from ministry and look for another career. This has been a blessed journey for me and the greatest privilege a son could ever hope to enjoy.

My father's story would be incomplete if not for my mother. Her story runs alongside and is intertwined with his. Mom has been Dad's partner, inspiration, and most devoted follower, sustaining him with tireless prayer support for over sixty years. Truly, the two have become one. I would hope someday that Mom would tell her story too, for it is one of great suffering, tremendous courage, and ultimate victory through the name of Jesus. She is a woman who has lived her faith in determined obedience to God—and is probably the godliest person I know.

I am pleased to invite you to pull up a chair and listen with me as my father tells the story of his life. This book is presented to you with the prayer that what you read will help you to see how God's grace is at work in your life and that everything you have gone through in the past, or are going through in the present, fits perfectly into God's will and that it is preparation for something else.

Chuck Smith, jr.

MARCH 2009

CHAPTER ONE

IF YOU HAD ASKED ME in my junior year of high school what I planned to do with my life, I would have given you a ready and confident answer: "I'm going to help people and make a decent living at the same time. I'm going to be a doctor." My determination was written all over my class schedule. In preparation for a premed degree, I had loaded it with science classes—biology, physiology, and chemistry. I had chosen a destination, unfurled a ten-year map, then highlighted all the routes I intended to take to reach my goal: an affluent surgeon in the service of God.

The problem with trying to predict the future, of course, is that we're blind to the obstacles placed along the path ahead. Plans have an unpleasant habit of going awry. No matter how often you scrutinize the map, trace your route, and dream of what you will see along the journey, you can't foresee the detours that await you.

The well-ordered future I had envisioned at sixteen instead became a confusing maze of sharp turns and dead ends. Some of the events I endured alone in my single years, as well as those I weathered later with my wife, Kay, seemed pointless and frustrating at the time. Yet looking back now, I can see the necessity of every unwanted experience. Only in retrospect am I able to connect the dots and marvel at God's ability to maneuver, prepare, and shape me for what *He* had in mind. From my birth—truly, even prior to my birth— there was a profound and specific purpose for my life, but it was not to be of my choosing. My course was guided by a greater wisdom.

Sometimes God guides us through thunderous events. Most often He uses quiet means—smaller moments, private pains, or the hush of a spontaneously whispered prayer offered up in a desperate plea. It was the latter that molded my life, before I'd even drawn one breath. To understand that, you need to know the story of Virginia.

Just prior to my birth, when the Smith family consisted of my parents, Charles and Maude, and my older sister, Virginia, the subject of church was not a unifying topic. My parents were not able to come to an agreement about religion. Dad had been raised in an upper middle-class Presbyterian home and chose to stay true to those roots. But he had also become disillusioned by some financial decisions made by church leaders while he was an elder, and as a result, his church attendance was sporadic and passionless.

Mom went to church regularly, walking a few blocks each Sunday to a Baptist church. But on occasion she ventured into the Pentecostal church that was nearer to their home. She enjoyed the livelier music she heard ringing from its windows, and the Pentecostal preacher's faith in God seemed stronger than that of her other pastor. Those Pentecostal folks still believed in miracles and divine healing.

And so when my sister contracted spinal meningitis, and the cool washcloths and the rocking and singing couldn't stave off her seizures—and the inevitable stilling of her breath—Mom picked up Virginia's limp body and ran next door to the Pentecostal parsonage.

The preacher took one look at Virginia in Mom's arms and steered them both into the church building. "Only God can save your daughter," he said. Then he told my mother to get her eyes off Virginia and put them on the Lord. He told her to pray, and said that if she wanted to see God intervene, she had better fully devote her life to Him.

My mother went a step further. She vowed that if He would spare and fully heal Virginia, then Mom would dedicate her life to Christian service.

My father was unaware of the drama unfolding on the floor of the Pentecostal church. In fact, he was out earning extra money for the family by playing in a pool tournament when Virginia had her seizure. But word reached him that his daughter had stopped breathing. He ran first to their apartment, where someone told him that Mom had carried Virginia's body to the church next door. Intending to scoop her up and take her straight to the hospital, Dad ran to the church. But when he entered the sanctuary and saw

Virginia's lifeless body lying on the floor, he fell on his knees next to Mom and cried out to God. And while Mom was offering up her vow and Dad was pleading for a miracle, Virginia was healed.

The miracle of my sister's recovery changed my father. In what must have been one of the most dramatic conversions of the decade, Dad turned his life over to the Lord. But he did not merely become a church member. Rather, he became a true believer who conscientiously lived for Jesus every day for the rest of his life.

Mom never forgot her vow. She determined that no matter what else she did with her life, she would fulfill her promise. In June of 1927, just two months after Virginia's ordeal, I was born. Though she fully intended to dedicate her own life to God—and did—she also felt an urging to present this fresh, new life to Him. At my birth she prayed, "Lord, I am going to fulfill my promise to You through my son."

Not wanting to influence my decision regarding my life's work and devotion to God, my mother never told me about the deal she made with God. But she never forgot nor abandoned it either. Without explicitly nudging me toward some kind of ministry, she began preparing me for the day she was certain would arrive—the day when God would call me into His service.

From my earliest memories, Mom taught me to memorize Scripture. If she was hanging laundry on the clothesline outside and I was playing nearby, she would have me recite the verses I had learned the day or week before. The same was true when she pushed me in the swing, or prepared dinner, or walked with me to the store. She turned Bible memorization into a game, and we played that game together until it melted into the rhythm of my climbing, hopping, jumping, and running. The Bible became as familiar to me as childhood axioms like, "Look both ways before crossing the street." Scripture was so ingrained in my mind that I could not imagine a world where the heavens did not declare the glory of God or where the Word had not become flesh and dwelt among us.

When I reached the age of four, Mom taught me to read. While she was folding or ironing clothes, she would have me read to her from the Bible. If I came to a word I could not pronounce, she would ask me to spell it out for her. If I did not know a letter, I would describe it for her, such as when I told her that a 'v' looked like "an upside-down tent," and so on.

Every night Mom read from the Bible for our bedtime stories. Those biblical characters became my heroes. More than heroes, they were friends—people I knew and among whom I lived. I fought the Philistines with Samson and trudged through the wilderness with Moses. But most of all I ran with David.

Before I entered elementary school I could name and spell all the books of the Bible. As I grew, church provided more exposure to the Bible and gave me experience in leadership, public speaking and choir training. During one period in school, I even took voice lessons to improve my singing ability, never guessing at how those exercises would serve me many years later. Each opportunity was preparation, but I was oblivious back then to the plans God had for my life.

* * * * *

No casual observer of my childhood would have guessed that God had placed a calling on my life. Life was simple in my hometown of Ventura, California, and my days were spent in all the same activities as other boys my age.

Back in the early years of my life, Ventura was a small beach town, and it remained quiet and untouched until the 1970s when the four-lane Ventura Highway was finally built. Our closest neighboring community of any size was Santa Barbara, accessible by a risky road that ran along the beach. Only a few decades earlier, people using that road would have had to stop at several points to wait for the tide to go out so they could continue their journey over the wet sand.

Ventura was linked to Los Angeles approximately sixty miles to the south by a small, primitive road that required a lot of winding, uphill driving through the coastal mountains—a slow and difficult journey. We were separated from beach communities to the south, because no roads had been cut through the rugged terrain along the Pacific Coast. Even today, Highway 1 veers several miles inland from Malibu before it reaches Ventura.

Ventura's relative isolation meant that we had long stretches of sandy beaches all to ourselves. I found myself drawn to the ocean almost every day. After school I would frequently grab my fishing pole and walk down to the beach. There I would dig up soft-shelled crabs for bait, then surf fish while wading in the water up to my knees. Sometimes I would hook a shovelnose shark and fight with it just for the sport. The corbina I often caught would be fried up by Mom and served to us for dinner.

Not far off the coast lie the Channel Islands. My friends and I sometimes boated over to Anacapa Island where we fished for rock cod. The water around Ventura and the islands was always clear and perfect for snorkeling. Although board surfing had not yet taken California by storm as it would in the '50s and '60s, we spent a lot of time in the ocean and learned how to bodysurf, enjoying the sheer pleasure of being carried by the waves to the shore.

The first white American settlers in Ventura were mostly interested in drilling for oil, but they and others soon discovered that the luxuriant soil of Ventura was excellent for farming. Fortunately for the dreamers who came to California during the gold rush, farmers discovered that the land surrounding Ventura yielded an excellent citrus crop. Those citrus farmers were the ones who truly struck gold, for the oranges and lemons they grew could cure the scurvy contracted by many of the gold diggers.

Our own bit of wealth grew in the walnut orchards that backed up to our house. After the trees had been harvested, we would go through the orchard gathering the walnuts they had missed. We then spread them out on the flat roof of our garage and left them to dry in the sun. The technology used to dry walnuts artificially changes the taste drastically. Oven-dried walnuts cannot come close to those that are sun-dried, and until you try one that's been dried naturally, you'll never know how delicious a walnut can really taste. Once dried, we'd shell the nuts and give them to Mom who would use them in all sorts of recipes. If you have not already discovered this truth, then you might as well learn it from me: When you look back on a long life, your best memories will be attached to events and pleasures that cost you absolutely nothing.

For the sheer beauty and grandeur of God's creation, you could not hope to experience much more than what we enjoyed every day in Ventura. Sunsets over the liquid horizon were always beautiful and no two were ever exactly the same. The ceaseless motion of the ocean's surface—from writhing swells with white-capped peaks to a flat and deceptively serene seascape—revealed different moods, shifting in just a few hours from angry violence, to brooding darkness, to the joyful celebration of life itself that was joined by pelicans and cormorants, the ever-present gulls and occasional snowy egret, and even bottlenose dolphins that surfaced from time to time not more than a hundred yards offshore. The ocean has a lesson to impart every time a person comes near, so long as they have ears to hear. "The voice of the Lord is upon the waters," no less today than when the psalmist heard Him speak centuries ago (Psalm 29:3).

Other than some prohibitions related to the peculiarities of our denomination, I was like any other kid—curious, mischievous, sometimes good as gold, and sometimes disobedient. I went through all the normal phases of boyhood, including chasing butterflies, climbing trees, building soapbox race cars, delivering newspapers, and playing with BB guns. Like other kids my age, I learned the value of a dollar while our family scrimped through the Great Depression. I experienced the mixture of fear and excitement when we'd have to rush through the house, turning off all the lights, as air raid sirens blared in the night during World War II.

My father, Charles, was a wonderful man. From childhood to this day I have thought of him with high regard and deep affection. Dad had a sincere love for strangers and a fearless commitment to telling anyone who crossed his path about salvation through Jesus Christ. In him, I had a superlative model of what Christian hospitality and personal evangelism should look like.

More than once, Dad's open-house policy nearly got our family into trouble—like the time we took a convict into our home, fresh out of prison. We later discovered he had been released by mistake. He was quite a character, but like many others, he came to faith in God through Dad's witness.

On another occasion when Dad was working in sales for the gas company, in the middle of his pitch he realized his client needed Jesus. Dad changed the direction and content of his spiel and presented the gospel to this wealthy and powerful business owner. The client, however, was not at all inclined toward Christianity and with a barrage of expletives let Dad know that he wanted nothing to do with religion. He berated Dad, told him he was a loser, and said the gas company should fire him because he could not possibly be a good salesman if he went around preaching religion.

Dad came home that afternoon feeling dejected, but quickly changed his attitude when he saw me and my brother, Paul, waiting to bring him with us to a high school football game. Just before we walked out the door, Dad trifled through the day's mail and found a letter from the Servel Electrolux Refrigerator Company notifying him that he had been awarded the top salesman in the nation that year and would soon receive a number of prizes along with a generous bonus. Dad stuffed the letter in his coat pocket and we drove off to the football game.

The stadium was packed but we spotted some empty seats near the top. After we made our way up the steps and sat down, my father noticed the man sitting in front of us was the same client who only an hour earlier had threatened to report him to the gas company and have him fired. They saw and recognized each other, briefly locked eyes, but said nothing. Dad nonchalantly reached into his coat pocket, pulled out the letter and handed it to the man, who read it and then muttered under his breath, "Well, I'll be darned!" Handing the letter back to Dad, he said, "Be in my office first thing tomorrow morning and we'll sign a contract."

Being a big fan of pro-football and baseball, Dad encouraged me in sports and showed up at almost all my games. In fact, Dad stood by my brothers and me in any manly pursuit that interested us, because he was convinced that if a man was going to fulfill his service to God, he would have to demonstrate masculine strength and courage. But Dad was also a gentleman and taught us respect for authority, women—and above all, God. The large crowd that came to Dad's funeral was a tribute to how deeply he was loved by many people.

But Dad was also fragile at times, which was perhaps a residual trauma of his experiences in the military during the First World

War. At times he became overly anxious about our circumstances, and would act out of fear before he had the chance to stop and think.

I remember one Christmas when we hit hard times and Dad could not afford to purchase any presents for the family. Having been raised in an affluent home where Christmas was always a big deal, our financial distress proved to be too much for him. He had a breakdown of sorts and could not get out of bed for several days.

Concerned over Dad's health, I climbed on my bike and rode through several neighborhoods selling new subscriptions for the newspaper I delivered. People must have been feeling extra generous, because I earned enough money that by Christmas morning I was able to put gifts under the tree for everyone in the family.

That was the most severe episode of Dad's anxiety I had ever witnessed. But other times, when his worry did not break him, it still drove him to self-defeating rumination and poor judgment. In those times, Mom was the rock. Her faith and devotion to God were a constant example to us. At night, the last thing I heard was Mom reading the Bible or praying out loud in the living room, and each morning I awoke to the comforting sound of her prayers.

My life was shaped by the faith of my parents, and because of their love for me and for God, I didn't doubt His existence or the truth of His Word. Still, I had no aspirations of being a minister. The thought never crossed my mind, nor do I remember a time in my youth when the ministry appealed to me. The ministers I knew were sincere, devoted men, but their lifestyle held no attraction to me. Surgeons, on the other hand, worked daily at the doorstep of life and death and had a skill that could determine on which side of the threshold their patient would land. And so, once the notion to become a doctor took root in my mind, all else fled. I centered all my attention and energy on making that future my reality. I felt certain I'd discovered my life's calling. And perhaps because I was so preoccupied with my own dreams, I missed the clues God left for me along the way, clues to the plan He had established before my birth. When I finally did see that plan, it took me by surprise. But God had been working it out all along.

Proverbs 19:21 makes a simple statement about God's will versus our own: "Many are the plans in a man's heart, but it is the Lord's purpose that prevails" (NIV). Few people learn God's will for their life in an instant revelation. Few stand before a burning bush and learn their God-given destiny. Instead, if we give ourselves to God's desires each morning and then move into what the day requires of us, somehow through our ordinary circumstances He prepares us and takes us into His will. For most of us, the best vantage point for understanding God's will for us is from that place at the end of our lives where we look back and see the clues we missed along the way. But God sees the end from the beginning.

I had no idea that my life was laid in God's hands at birth. But when I look back now it is clear to me that God's first word to Jeremiah, with slight modification, could have been said to me and to every other believer: "Before I formed you in the womb I knew you; and before you came forth out of the womb I sanctified you, and I ordained you a prophet unto the nations" (Jeremiah 1:5).

2

CHAPTER TWO

Even the most momentous days usually begin like every other ordinary morning. The first time God rattled my world, I received no advanced warning. God did not send an announcement the night before or wake me from a sound sleep to say, "Later today I will ask you to make the most important decision of your life. I will also do a work in your heart so that you are compelled to say yes. Afterward, you will follow Me into the unknown."

But that is basically what happened, and I didn't see it coming.

*   *   *   *   *

That particular Sunday night did not feel momentous. In fact, we had just returned home from a family vacation to Bass Lake and we were all feeling that post-vacation lethargy that settles in when the fun is behind you.

Bass Lake, located in the wooded forests of the Sierra Nevada Mountain Range near Yosemite, California, is postcard beautiful and a favorite family spot. Some of my most memorable moments are framed by the pine forest surrounding the lake, the breathtaking sight of El Capitan jutting 3,000 vertical feet into the sky, and the exquisite artistry of our Creator as we hiked to Half Dome. On this trip, we had camped near the lake, toured Yosemite Valley, jumped from bridges into the frigid water of swollen streams, fished for dinner, and slept under the stars. The trip was wonderful, if exhausting. I hadn't realized how tiring it was for my parents until, after arriving home and unpacking the car, my father tossed me the car keys and said, "Son, you can drive your sister to church tonight. Mom and I need to rest up for this coming week."

My parents never skipped a church service. In fact, only in the most severe cases of illness (or death) would my parents miss a Sunday morning, Sunday night, or Wednesday night service. But I didn't question him on this. At fourteen, I liked driving. Dad had decided a few months earlier that it would work to his benefit if I could drive the family car. The streets of Ventura in those days were far less dangerous than city streets today, and with the proper paperwork, parents could request early licenses for their children. All things considered, he thought I was responsible enough to be entrusted with this privilege, so he filed the necessary forms and I got my license.

It came in handy in this instance. Leaving our younger brothers behind, Virginia and I climbed in the car and headed off to church. I don't want to give the impression that I thought it was great fun going to church or that I could hardly wait for the preacher to begin his sermon. Attending church was something I took for granted; it was simply what we did—a family tradition—and neither Dad nor Mom ever suggested that we had a choice in the matter.

As far as I was concerned, if I had to be at church then I would participate and make the most of it. When in Sunday school, I sang the songs, memorized the Bible verses, listened to the stories, and answered the questions. But by the time I was a teenager, my relationship to the church changed slightly because we did not have much of a youth group. Having made the assumption that I had jumped through every hoop our church had expected of me, I was sort of spiritually coasting through that time of my life, focusing more on school and sports than on church activities.

Generally on Sunday nights I sat in the back row with a couple of my friends from high school. We were not obnoxious and did not draw attention to ourselves, but we did goof off some, perfecting ways to quietly pass the time during the sermon—by doodling, seeing who could hold his breath the longest, or having a handshake contest in which we squeezed the other guy's hand until our fingers turned blue and one of us had to surrender.

I can't recall much about that particular Sunday night service. I don't remember the hymns we sang, which text the pastor chose for the sermon, or even what the preacher said about it. I suppose the songs were too familiar to stand out, and as usual, the sermon was not interesting enough to catch (or require) my attention. These regularly repeated activities tend to blend into the ordinary backdrop of all those years I spent going to church, and on this occasion they had little relation to what happened to me that night.

The tradition of our denomination was to conclude every service with an invitation to the congregation, asking people to leave their seats and make their way to the front of the church to meet with God. A number of evangelical churches observe this tradition, but in Pentecostal churches the altar call was honed to an art form, where it became the high point of the service, the climax for which everything else was preliminary. Sometimes people were invited forward if they needed divine healing or wanted to receive a spiritual gift. Most of the time, however, we were urged to come and be saved or rededicate our lives to God—in case the initial dedication did not take.

I don't remember one word from the pitch the preacher gave on this particular evening, but something strange happened when the service reached that critical moment of invitation. Was there something different about the program that night? Had the pastor altered something, or was the music new? I don't remember anything unusual about that service. As well as I can recall, that Sunday night was no different from any other Sunday night and I likely missed most of the sermon while participating in a breath-holding contest in the back row. But when the pastor asked us to respond to God by getting up and coming forward, the words got through to me. Gripped by a strong conviction, I was compelled to stand.

Before I walked forward to meet with God, I turned to my friend, Robert. I assumed he felt the same sense of urgency, so I said, "Come on, let's go up front."

But he looked at me as if I were joking, then shook his head and said, "Nah."

"Well, I'm going forward," I said. I stood up and walked the short distance from my seat in the back, down the aisle to the front, and stood there with the pastor. No one paid much attention to me because it was expected that we would all make an obligatory trip to the altar once in a while. But for me, as I went forward, I stepped into a real, spiritual encounter.

I cannot define my experience that night, and would probably spoil the moment if I tried. I prefer to let it remain a mystery. All that mattered was that I knew God had called me to Himself and I could not decline. Still shaking when I returned home, I went into my parents' room and told them what happened. As I remember, they were pleased but did not make a big deal about it. The experience was mine and no one else would ever be able to appreciate it as much as I did.

Looking back on that night and what happened between God and me, the timing was perfect. My mother's determination to keep her promise to God had a great influence upon my mind and heart though at that time it was unknown to me, but her devotion could take me only so far. From there I had to find my own way into God's will. I needed my own relationship with Him, and for this to happen, He had to build a bridge to my heart. Like most young

CHUCK SMITH: A MEMOIR OF GRACE

men, during the developmental stage of my teenage years, I needed to pull away from my mother in order to become my own person. It's a necessary part of the process in becoming a man. At critical points, the Lord intervened and supplanted the role of my mother by doing His own shaping and molding work in me. I wanted to become a man; He wanted to make me a man of God.

Did my life radically change after that uncanny evening of awakening? Was I determined from that moment on to give God every minute of my day, enter the ministry, forsake all worldly pursuits and live in strict obedience to Him? Not really. I was the same young man who enjoyed playing football, dreamed of becoming a surgeon, and looked forward to a life of comfortable affluence and charitable giving. The experience did not make a radical difference in my life, and as far as my family and friends were concerned, there may not have been any noticeable difference. But the experience happened. I knew it was real, it moved and marked me, and I would never forget it.

It may seem anticlimactic to say that I woke up the next day without having undergone a total transformation. But the fact that I cannot remember any significant effect of the experience on my heart or mind reinforces a theme that stretches over my whole life: Everything is preparation for something else. Even those highly emotional or spiritual events that carry us heavenward on a Sunday night, but quickly fade in the intense light of real life, prepare us for something. The meaning of that event was not linked to anything that happened in the days, weeks, or months to follow. Nevertheless, I have carried it in my heart ever since. God is real,

He loves me, He wants me, and that night He called me. For better or for worse, I told Him, "Yes."

The step I took toward the altar was a very important first step. Once taken, I stood on a different plane than I had prior to that night. No, I could not discern the difference of life on this new level, but God Himself took me there. That in itself made me ready for the next challenge. As Jesus said, faithfulness in the small things is rewarded with greater things.

*   *   *   *   *

Between my freshman and sophomore years in high school, we moved from Ventura to Santa Ana, California. At that time, Orange County lived up to its name and to this day when our orange tree blooms every spring, its fragrance takes me back to those formative teenage years. Orange County was still covered in farmland in the early 1940s, even though the rapid development of Southern California was well underway. Santa Ana was not a big city nor densely populated like Los Angeles, but it was still much larger and busier than the rural community of Ventura.

After making the move, one of the first things my parents did was to find us a family church associated with the denomination of the Ventura church. We received a warm welcome on our first visit and easily settled into our new spiritual home. Our routine of church services gobbled up several hours every week, but my primary concerns were still centered in academics and athletics.

During the summer of my sixteenth birthday, our pastor announced a camping program hosted by our church's denomination. As it turned out, I was the only person from our church's youth group to attend.

In 1943, with the Los Angeles Basin as yet untouched by smog, the San Bernardino Mountains provided all the wonder of nature in its pristine glory within a couple of hours from home. Camp Radford belonged to the county of Los Angeles and was nestled among towering pine trees in a densely wooded forest nearly 7,000 feet above sea level. Every winter several feet of snow covered the camp, and during the summer it gurgled with the sound of engorged streams.

In those days, the average teenager did not expect summer camp to be a week at a posh resort. Camp was camp. Wooden picnic benches served for dining tables in the mess hall, which had screened windows but no glass. The modern miracle of indoor plumbing had yet to find its way to Radford, so one of the first facilities to locate upon arriving at camp was the small wood-slat shack with a crescent moon on the door. The first person to enter the cabin after its long season of being sealed against the winter was accosted with a musty odor that still evokes a flood of camp memories whenever I smell it. I always pitied the kids with asthma and allergies, because gaps between the logs in those rustic cabins allowed even the slightest draft to chill us at night and choke us with dust during the day.

The week itself included typical outdoor activities during the day, a spiritual moment around a fire ring each evening, followed by a service in the chapel. In the course of a week, camp would range from light-hearted silliness to deadly serious sermons meant to inspire—or coerce—a new commitment to Jesus or a fresh experience of God's Spirit. Much of the spirituality to which we were exposed was designed to stir the heartstrings. Now and again, however, there were brilliant exceptions.

God has always used nature to awaken my heart and He has approached me through the wonder of a verdant forest, crystal clear stream, and a stellar jay's scolding more times than I can remember. So given the splendor of my surroundings, it was no surprise that I found God near to me at camp. At times too, the music of our worship seemed to merge with the smoke of the fire ring and waft heavenward, an offering pleasing to God and acceptable in His sight.

But the moment that was most special to me came at the end of every day. Even now I can close my eyes and feel the pleasure that swept over me as I pulled my sleeping bag up to my neck just after lights out. Of course, a camper is never so vulnerable as when night descends, never so prone to bouts of loneliness, irrational fears, and the creeping up of those spooky feelings of the divine Spirit that haunted old Abram when he laid out his sacrifice before Yahweh (Genesis 15:12).

But good things filled my mind too. Thoughts evoked by the nature lessons, Bible studies, and evangelical appeals during the day would stir the conscience in those moments just before falling asleep. It was a perfect time for reflection, listening to God's voice in the inner person, and finding spiritual reassurance in Jesus.

CHUCK SMITH: A MEMOIR OF GRACE

Loudspeakers which hung from various poles, eaves and branches around the campgrounds were used to sound revelry in the morning and make important announcements during the day. But when all the campers were on their bunks and the camp went dark, the staff would play a few songs over the PA system, and every night the last song to be blared into our sleepy heads was "The Lord's Prayer."

I do not really remember singing "The Lord's Prayer" in our church. The worship pendulum in our denomination swung from rousing to schmaltzy. The "Our Father" was something one would expect to hear in one of the "high church" liturgies. But being a music lover by nature—and a violin player by threat of force—I became enthralled with the melody that had been wrapped around the words given to us by our Lord for addressing the Father "who is in secret," and presenting to Him all of our needs, from the daily and mundane, to the critical forgiveness of trespasses and infinite grandeur of His eternal kingdom and will. "For Thine is the kingdom, and the power, and the glory, for-ev-er. Ah-a-men."

*   *   *   *   *

Each of us in a lifetime will probably encounter only a few people whose love for Jesus is so sincere, whose relationship with the Scripture is so profound, and whose prayer is so deep that conversing with them is a spiritual exercise in itself. Harold Chalfant, the director of the camp, was such a person to me. His speech and his life lifted my heart toward God.

When the Pentecostal movement emerged in the early twentieth century, it found its native soil in the lower classes of American society. Many Pentecostal believers did not trust theologians who in their opinion did not have the "Holy Ghost." Therefore, our denomination was not known for having many men or women of outstanding brilliance or education. The few leaders who were actual scholars stood out from the rest of our preachers and professors. Chalfant, however, was a true genius and I was immediately drawn to his light. When he spoke, I hung on every word.

When it came to the art of preaching, he was a master. His voice rose and fell with the pitch and resonance of a philharmonic orchestra, his down-home style was enhanced by the quality of his eloquence, and he could pour so much emotion into each word he spoke that we couldn't help but feel what he felt and be carried wherever he took us. True to Scripture, fervent for God, and a powerful communicator, Harold Chalfant had us on the edge of our seats.

One evening, after taking us on a breathtaking journey, Chalfant concluded his message with a simple poem that in some ways embodied what Paul had said in Philippians 1:21, "For to me to live is Christ, and to die is gain." "Only one life," Chalfant intoned, "will soon be past; only what's done for Christ will last." The impact of those fourteen words on my heart was not due to the poem, but to the context he had created prior to quoting the poem. I heard in his words the challenge to step up to a life that was not devoured by short-term pursuits, but rather devoted to achievements that would last for eternity. I learned from this passionate and outstanding man that a person could live for God and yet have a meaningful life.

In a talk Chalfant gave later that same week, I heard God's call in another statement that is so simple as to sound silly. But again, it was the context of his message from Scripture that framed these words and gave them their force in my heart and mind. "Everyone is a fool for someone or something," he said, "so why not be a fool for Christ?" I heard him say that the sort of passion worthy of consuming one's whole life is found not in the ambition to acquire wealth, control a large corporation, wield power, or stun others with one's intellectual prowess, but to walk with Jesus Christ, carrying on His work in the lives of others at whatever the cost. "Not my will but Thine be done," I heard Jesus pray, and Chalfant invited me to kneel next to the Lord and repeat that prayer with Him. Through these two moments I experienced in Chalfant's sermons, a new perspective determined my life's course.

Away from the city, with the words of the Bible and various speakers churning inside, I looked for a quiet place where I could sort things out. Up until that week at camp, I knew what I wanted to do with my life. Sports had taken on a significant role for me and I had hoped to obtain at least a partial scholarship to play football for a university where I could begin courses for a premed major. To me, becoming a surgeon seemed like the best way to enjoy a good life while helping others at the same time.

But sitting alone under a pine tree, I found myself reflecting on what it would be like if Jesus were Lord of my life. Until then I had always been grateful that He was my Savior and Protector, but I had not given much thought to the significance of calling Him, "Lord" and really meaning it. It occurred to me that if I became a doctor, the best I could do for people would be to improve their health for a short time. But eventually they would still die, and then what? They would enter an eternal realm for which I could not prepare them.

The wind whistled through the pine needles overhead and I looked up into clouds drifting across a blue sky framed by green branches. At that moment I felt my heart being called to Bible college where I could prepare for a life of service to God and His people.

When I returned home from camp, I plucked up my courage to let my mother know that I was scrapping my plans to become a doctor. From now on my course would be the pursuit of God and the building of His kingdom. I had imagined Mom responding with deep disappointment, and the last thing I wanted to do was to hurt her in any way. But God came first and I figured that she would eventually understand. To my surprise, however, she smiled and said, "If that is what you believe God wants you to do, then your father and I will stand by you."

She had never mentioned to me the oath she had made to God at my birth. She didn't want her will to influence my course. Instead, she wanted God to draw me His direction. And even at this point, when I was sharing with her the conviction God had placed on my heart, she still did not tell me about her vow. It was only later that I realized she had purposely minimized her reaction to my news. This was the critical moment for which she had waited all those years of my childhood and adolescence. Even then she decided to wait and see if this was a real life-altering decision or merely a case of short-lived bravado so typical of youthful enthusiasm.

*   *   *   *   *

Our life is a story that we write as we journey through a series of episodes, with each one leaving its impression on us and slightly altering the direction or manner in which we move forward. Although we are writing our story every day, we do not determine what happens in each episode. All we are given is the freedom to decide how we will respond to what happens—God controls the plot.

Still, we are not merely along for the ride. We carry a certain amount of responsibility in choosing the actions that unfold in particular scenes, how we respond in a moment of opportunity or disappointment, and whether or not we step up to the challenges and risks that come to us. Our attitude toward any particular event in life can be, "This is good," "This is not good," or "This is meaningless." We have to learn along the way to resist the negative attitudes; such as doubt, frustration, and/or despair that arise within the context of a specific event. We have to learn to see how our story is attached to a larger story, the story of God's work in human history starting from the time of Adam to the closing scene of this present age. From this point of view, we can always adopt an attitude of faith and hope in the present and for the future.

We cannot help but sometimes misinterpret the meaning of our immediate circumstances. Like Jacob, who learned that a mighty leader in Egypt demanded his youngest son to journey with his older brothers if they were to buy food for their survival, we lament over discouragement, bad news, and setbacks. "All these things are against me," the old man whined (Genesis 42:36). But Jacob was wrong. He reached his mistaken conclusion from the events that unfolded in just this one difficult episode. His vantage point did not allow him to see into the distance. His complaint was, in fact, exactly the opposite of what was actually happening to him. "All things were working together for good" on his behalf and for the welfare of his family (Genesis 45:4-8, 13).

We cannot read our life's plot from one event or episode. We cannot say whether an event is working to help us accomplish our goal or is threatening to sabotage it. But we can know this: If we are surrendered to God, all things work together for our good (Romans 8:28). No single moment in our life stands in isolation from all the other moments. What doesn't make sense today is explained tomorrow, what we painfully learn this year is an education we will appreciate next year, and everything is preparation for something else.

God does not push us into His will. Rather, He invites us to come and follow Him, walk with Him, trust Him, choose Him. Every moment is an invitation, an opportunity, a choice. Whether we go forward with God or not is our moment-to-moment decision.

The same week I returned home from camp, our pastor asked if I would be willing to become the youth director for our church. The distance between that pine tree where I decided to enter ministry and this opportunity closed frightfully fast. How could I turn down his request? The following year when I returned to summer camp, I brought 140 kids with me. Somehow these kids had caught my excitement over this new relationship with the Lord, realized it began for me at camp, and decided they wanted to taste it for themselves.

There is no reason to glamorize my work as a youth director, because for the most part it consisted of planning our Sunday night meetings. For some reason, the Foursquare denomination chose to use military metaphors in the development of their youth ministries, so we were "Crusaders for Christ." Bear in mind that the Foursquare headquarters were founded about a decade after WWI and the church was very active in home-base support of servicemen and the war effort during WWII when warfare was very much on the minds of North Americans. Also, the founder of the denomination, Aimee Simple McPherson, seemed enamored with the idea of spiritual warfare and was probably hyperliteral in her interpretation of 1 John 2:14, "I have written unto you, young men, because you are strong, and the Word of God abides in you, and you have overcome the wicked one."

We would hold contests to see who could locate Bible verses first, referring to these exercises as "sword drills"—the Bible being "the sword of the Spirit" referred to in Ephesians 6:17. With Bibles closed, we would be given a verse to find and we were told to "present arms," at which point we would hold out our Bibles with the binding toward us and the pages facing away. Then, when the command came to "Charge!" we would begin turning pages as fast as we could in search of the mystery verse. Whoever found it first would stand and read it aloud. Generally, when all the verses were read, they were thematically linked and related to that evening's lesson.

Other planning included choosing which choruses we would sing and arrange for guest speakers. The guests usually told the story of how they came to faith in Christ or experienced a miraculous healing. Almost every speaker spent at least a little time exhorting us to live decent and moral Christian lives.

We spent part of each evening divided into two teams and we were given Bible quizzes. Points were awarded for giving the right answers and by the end of the contest a winning team and a losing team were determined. This particular activity turned out to be one more way that God strangely prepared me for an important revelation that came to me at a later stage in my journey.

Rather than ransack my Bible each week in search of difficult questions for our quizzes, the pastor gave me a Bible quiz book in which questions and answers were already available for meetings such as ours. Seeing that I was generally the moderator for the quizzes, and therefore the one asking the questions and awarding points for the right answers, I inadvertently memorized every question and answer in the book. This was sort of a fringe benefit to my biblical education that turned to my advantage in a way I could have never anticipated.

Everything is preparation for something else.

*   *   *   *   *

Like many other young people in my church, Bible reading was not a high priority for me. Instead of reading the Bible all the way through, we read select passages, generally from the Psalms and the Gospels. We also had our favorite verses that were drawn from the letters of Paul. Most of the sermons we heard were topical sermons developed from just one or two verses and supported by several other verses from different parts of the Bible. Sometimes we were given the whole context from which the verse was taken, but I cannot remember ever hearing a Bible study that took us through an entire book.

Nevertheless, because God knew my calling would be to teach His people the Bible from cover to cover, He kept me in contact with Scripture. First, my mother had me memorizing verses, then my Sunday school classes and pastor's sermons refreshed my mind in the Word, and then I spent time preparing for my youth leader ministry each week. In one way or another, the Bible was constantly before me.

Whatever is done for God in this world does not leave much for a man or woman to brag about. At most, "we are unprofitable servants: we have done that which was our duty to do" (Luke 17:10). The reason we have to forfeit bragging rights is because all we can do is allow God's Word to enter us and be what it is—life-giving and creative.

Think of this: "The Word of God is quick, and powerful, and sharper than any two-edged sword" (Hebrews 4:12). The word "quick" in old English means "alive" or "living." The Scriptures are not dead words imprisoned in ink on a page, but like the first human, they are God-breathed—literally inspired—and God uses them to enter people, turn them toward Himself, and transform their lives.

Bible stories, memory verses, quizzes, and sword drills were like small seeds that God dropped into my heart, preparing me for the day when His Word would take over my life—and indeed, become my life and ministry.

3

CHAPTER THREE

Do you remember your senior year in high school? Some kids are excited about their future while others feel the pressure of trying to figure out what they'll do with the rest of their life after graduation. In my case, I was so eager to jump into the next phase of my life that I managed to graduate early. I now realize how naive I was to assume that my confident plans for the future would progress as I imagined. I knew God had called me to ministry and I never dreamed of going back on my commitment. Yet, at the same time, it seemed to me that God would be best served if I had at least a small measure of life experience and financial security under my belt. So I started the process of enlisting in the Air Force, passed their qualifying exam, and began mentally preparing myself for active duty. I figured that once I finished my stint in the service

I would have the means to pay my way through Bible college and be set for the future.

The winter prior to graduation, Dad talked me into riding up to Los Angeles with him to visit LIFE Bible College. To be honest, at seventeen years old I felt restless to do something physically demanding and mentally challenging. Athletic challenges and competition had always appealed to me and I had no desire to waste my youth. The idea of sitting in Bible classes six hours a day seemed like an intolerable misuse of my strength and energy.

When we arrived on campus, I learned that our former pastor in Ventura was the current dean of students for the Bible college. When we met with him, he asked what my plans were now that I had graduated. I told him I was headed for the Air Force and would return to attend Bible college after I served my time. Sounding sincerely concerned, he asked one simple question. "Why don't you put God first and see what happens?" For the next few weeks I could not shake his words or their grip on my heart.

In my mind, the Air Force was a way to move my life forward. But not only that, by joining voluntarily, I could choose my own branch of service. In January 1945 the WWII draft was still in force, which meant that I would likely be conscripted into active duty anyway. Joining before that would give me some control. But now the dean had thrown a complicating factor into my plans. Although my ultimate goal was to serve God, I had figured out a strategy that allowed me to do it my own way, on my own terms. It hadn't occurred to me that God not only desired my future service, He had His own plans as to how I would get there.

I couldn't shake the dean's question. After careful thought, I decided to let my future rest in God's hands. Like every other young man my age, I was registered for the draft and determined to go when called upon to serve my country. But while waiting, I began a correspondence course in biblical studies through LIFE Bible College. By the time I was able to attend classes on campus, the war was over and the draft was suspended. In the spring of 1945, I began my sophomore year at LIFE.

From the moment I entered the school I felt out of place, and my heart really hadn't settled into the Foursquare denomination. I am not critical of my alma mater, its philosophy, faculty, or the churches it serves. I received training—and much more—from many godly people I encountered during my years of ministry. I still hold many of them close to my heart—people who are still associated with the Foursquare Church and whose influence for Christ is obvious and undeniable. But belonging to that tradition was not the right fit for me.

From my point of view, the spiritual life I witnessed on campus had an overly emotional quality that sometimes led to impractical behavior. I have never doubted the fact that God still works miracles, and I have even seen a few firsthand. But the idea that miracles are as normal and frequent as the sun's rising and setting goes beyond my own experience and understanding of Scripture.

For example, I have never been frivolous with money—neither my own nor God's—yet I have seen some Christian leaders handle money or conduct business quite carelessly, expecting God to miraculously fund their work. It seems to me that biblical faith is rooted in common sense, such as we find in the wisdom revealed in the book of Proverbs. If I want to see a harvest of wheat, I must plant wheat seeds. To go to a fallow field and do no more than pray for a harvest is not faith, but folly.

Some of the spiritual themes of my college contrasted with my personality and my relationship with God. I doubted that the Spirit of God would inspire behavior that would make people look silly or out of control. That kind of behavior contradicted my idea of the way Jesus, Paul, or any of the disciples would have behaved. If anything, the Spirit made them more human, more stable and more in charge—not less.

The whole culture around campus and the sort of spirituality it produced felt foreign to me, which probably explains why I was the only one in my graduating class who was not "slain in the Spirit"[1] when I received my ordination. My parents were not too pleased with my apparent lack of spirituality, nor was the college president. When I didn't go down after receiving the gentle "nudge of the Spirit" he gave me, the president leaned in close and whispered, "You'd better go down on one knee, son." The only person there who was proud of me was Kay, my lovely and devoted wife. She knew I was not a rebel, but simply wished to be true to myself and the person God called me to be.

My concerns about the spirituality I witnessed on campus con-nected with a concern I had prior to entering Bible college and helped to clarify one of my central goals in ministry. Certain spokespersons for Christianity—men and women who were presented as models of Christian devotion—were rarely the type of individuals that inspire young men to follow in their footsteps. I could not imagine guys who played on my high school football team giving them the time of day. Frequently, the public figures who represented Christianity were past the prime of life, wore frumpy clothing, and would not have known "cool" if it fell out of the sky and landed on their heads. Some of them also adopted a spiritual demeanor with a marked feminine effect that my masculine brain and body would never be able to imitate.

It wasn't that I believed a model Christian leader had to be all brute strength, emotionless, an intellectual without a heart—or like one of our celebrated Christian athletes who is biblically clueless but famous for his body count on the field. Rather I felt like my friends and I needed a man's man to look up to, a hero of sorts who was strong and who could be tough, if need be, passionate and courageous, unafraid to stand alone, if necessary, and committed to defending his beliefs and community. It seemed that Christian leadership was lacking men who were virile as well as articulate.

In *The Abolition of Man*, C. S. Lewis takes to task certain scholars who tried to define manliness apart from passion, thus creating what he referred to as "men without chests." He accused them of hiding behind the pretense of being more intellectual because they were less emotional, but argued that their "heads are no bigger than ordinary: it is the atrophy of the chest beneath that makes them seem so." Lewis observed that Western society in the mid-twentieth century called for "more drive or dynamism or self-sacrifice or creativity" at the same time that it robbed men of the emotions that underlie those qualities. "In a sort of ghastly simplicity we remove the organ and demand the function." He ends his essay saying, "We make men without chests and expect of them virtue and enterprise. We laugh at honor and are shocked to find traitors in our midst. We castrate and bid the geldings be fruitful."[2]

My heart yearned to provide the world—and especially young men in the church—with a different model of Christian leader. A man of strength in every respect; character and fortitude, physical stamina and vitality, intelligence and breadth of mind. One of my greatest joys is that all through my many years of ministry, God has inspired a cadre of talented, smart, and energetic young men to join me in Christian service.

*   *   *   *   *

Given the combination of youthful idealism and chronic insecurity of eighteen- to twenty-three-year-olds, it is normal to witness a lot of posturing on Bible college campuses. LIFE had its share of super-spiritual students who let the rest of us know how frequently they retired to their rooms to pray, how many times they were slain in the Spirit, and how many hours they spent each day speaking in unknown tongues. Since the culture of the school (and denomination) encouraged this kind of one-upmanship, students tended to admire those who openly displayed their piety.

The college was divided between day school and night school students, which resulted in a natural, intramural rivalry. The faculty actively encouraged the two schools to try to outdo each other in their performance of academic, biblical, and spiritual activities.

This competitive challenge played into the desire of those who wished to demonstrate their superior biblical and spiritual depth. The whole contrivance of competitive programs in the Foursquare Church became an important factor in the events that led to my eventual departure from the denomination.

I remember one contest between the day and night schools particularly well. In this instance, the faculty had scheduled a showdown to determine which school had a better knowledge of the Bible. Both schools put together their teams and as it turned out, I was one of the students chosen to compete for the day school team.

Prior to the competition, our team met in a room behind the stage, where everyone except me felt it would be to our advantage to seek God's help in order to whomp the night school. "O Lord, help us win," they intoned.

I was the only one who refused to join in their prayers for victory. "What difference does it make who wins and what good will it do to pray if we're not already prepared?" I asked them. Oddly, my teammates thought we could win the contest by the miraculous intervention of God's Spirit rather than by reading the Bible. Baffled at my lack of spiritual depth, some soundly rebuked me. Others tried to quietly cast demons out of me.

When the first round of questions ended, I was the only student from the day school remaining in the competition. I don't recall how many rounds we had, but by the end of the contest I had single-handedly beat the night school's team.

I would love to say that all of my mother's influence in my early years and all those Bible verses I memorized in Sunday school had left their mark on me and that is why my biblical knowledge rose above every other student. Or it would be gratifying to convince myself that my commitment at summer camp really took hold of my life and gave me a deeper appreciation for the Scriptures than that of the other students. The truth, however, is that the college faculty who put together the contest used the very same quiz book I had used when I was the youth leader in my home church. Unbeknown to me or anyone else, I came into the competition better prepared than any other contestant. Before the first question was asked, I already knew the answer to every one. I decided, however, to keep this information to myself because my teammates—who prior to the contest were convinced I was pitifully unspiritual—were stupefied (and impressed) with my victory.

While working as a volunteer with the high school group in my church, there was no way for me to know that the groundwork was being laid for a contest I would enter in Bible college. Was this God's purpose for permitting the contest organizers to use the same quiz book I had used earlier? Was winning the contest the goal for which God had previously prepared me? Was it important to God that I won a Bible quiz?

No, God's concern was not my victory in the competition between the day and night schools. But the contest was symbolic of God's work in my life. Through it, I learned two important lessons.

First, I learned the importance of hiding God's Word in my heart. While my classmates prayed for a miraculous intervention, I was inclined to approach our challenge rationally. Afterward, the lesson was clear: to prepare yourself to face an unknown future, study the Scriptures now. No doubt troubles, hardships, and crises will arise for which you cannot prepare yourself beforehand, and God will always supply grace for those times. But God has revealed the Scripture to us and His desire is to work in our lives through His Word.

Secondly, I learned something about the theme of my life. It would be through my relationship with God's Word that I would leave my mark.

We sometimes find within Old Testament stories that an event's message and meaning are revealed in a key word or phrase. For example, the theme of "return" is stressed in the first chapter of Ruth. Naomi had to *return* to her homeland. Her widowed daughters-in-law intended to accompany her until she told them to *return* to the homes of their parents. Initially they refused and insisted on *returning* with her, but Naomi held her ground and told them again, two more times, to *return*. At that point one of her daughters-in-law kissed Naomi goodbye and *returned* to Moab. All of this highlighted Ruth's loyalty expressed in her famous speech, "Wherever you go, I will go" (Ruth 1:6-22 NKJV).

The author of Ruth makes this point by the simple repetition of a key word and does so without breaking the rhythm of the story. The message and meaning are embedded in the story. I believe we discover the message and meaning of our lives by living out our story. God repeats themes, places His blessing on a particular kind of endeavor, and reveals a pattern through the important turning points of our life's story so that we learn His will for us even as we live it. It pleases God to guide our lives by continuously giving us directions rather than giving us a map. He is with us always and wants us to be listening always.

*　*　*　*　*

The word "Pentecostal" is an indicator of what lies at the heart of this Christian movement. The day of Pentecost recorded in Acts 2 marked the fulfillment of Jesus' promise to the disciples that they would receive the promise of the Father and receive power after the Holy Ghost had come upon them (Luke 24:49; Acts 1:8). Pentecost had been the "Feast of Weeks" in Israel's religion, but was reinterpreted by the Christian community according to the miracle that occurred that day. For some biblical scholars, this event marks the birth of the church.

Defined by the phenomena that occurred on the day of Pentecost, Pentecostalism is event-oriented. Individual events include the baptism of the Holy Spirit, speaking in tongues (as on the day of Pentecost, Acts 2:4), divine healing, and other signs and wonders. Community events usually included public exhibitions of the supernatural working of the Holy Spirit, especially the so-called "sign gifts" in 1 Corinthians 12:7-10. Many Pentecostal Christians have been led to believe that the Spirit of God is not present in a meeting unless a miracle occurs.

In some Pentecostal churches pastors try to reach certain benchmarks each week including, "There was not a dry eye in the building" and "Everyone went forward that night." But if everyone "went forward" last Sunday evening, what are we to conclude if everyone does not go forward this week? If those benchmark effects determine the presence of the Spirit in a meeting, preachers find themselves faced with the temptation to move people emotionally by one means or another if it does not seem that the Spirit is moving them.

Another indicator of the Spirit's presence in the service was the "anointing" that rested on the preacher—meaning that the sermon was delivered with power that comes through the direct inspiration of God's Spirit. The anointing is sometimes measured by how many wise, clever, or funny statements the preacher makes. But more often than not, the "anointed preacher" is the animated preacher who trembles and shouts. A soft-spoken preacher obviously lacks the necessary gifts to meet Pentecostal requisites. I will always appreciate my professor who urged us not to mistake perspiration for inspiration. Sadly, he spoke with quiet confidence. Had he shouted, his students would have been more inclined to pay attention to him.

Of course, ministers cannot produce miracles in every service. What they can do, however, is blame the people in their congregations for the absence of the miraculous in those meetings. "There's not enough faith here tonight," the minister might proclaim, or "You haven't prayed through" or "Sin blocks the work of God" and so on. Or the preacher can attempt to produce a different sort of miracle—the miracle of a saved soul. Of the many reasons why saving sinners in every service made sense to Pentecostal ministers, the primary reason had to do with church growth. It was not difficult to convince church members of their duty to fulfill Jesus' last instruction to the disciples, referred to in Matthew's gospel, to go and evangelize the world.

The idea that a church meeting could serve to invite sinners to come to Jesus and meet Him at the altar depended entirely on the presence of sinners in those meetings. During the days of Aimee Simple McPherson, the Foursquare church, "Angelus Temple" in Los Angeles never lacked in unbelievers who wandered in off the street, curious to learn what the furor was about or drawn by the theatrical performances. Ms. McPherson arrived in Los Angeles as a tent evangelist who had traversed the states proclaiming the cross of Jesus to those who needed forgiveness. She continued doing so in Los Angeles and frequently saw a good number of the unsaved turn to God each week.

But away from Los Angeles, in rural communities where crowds did not line up at the doors of Foursquare churches waiting for services to begin, there was less of a likelihood that preachers would find outsiders in any of their services. In fact, many people were put off by the Foursquare name or its "holy roller" reputation because some thought it was a cult.

So local pastors in small churches entered their pulpits with well-prepared, soul-saving sermon notes in hand only to find that there was not a single sinner in the building. Well, if you can't save the ones you want, save the ones you're with. Preachers could still call sinners to the altar with slight modifications to the sermon. After all, if these people were *real* Christians, they would have brought their non-Christian neighbors with them to church that evening. Did they not care that the man or woman or child living next door was destined to a Christ-less eternity? How could they abandon those lost people to the flames of hell while they drove complacently to church? They obviously needed to come to the altar and repent.

And if we didn't learn all of this in our churches back home—Bible college drummed it into us. We were told repeatedly that the role of the church on earth is to evangelize the world. In fact, the acronym of our college, LIFE, stood for "Lighthouse of International Foursquare Evangelism," and prior to that name, which it received when it moved into the five-story building next to Angelus Temple, it was known as "Echo Park Evangelistic and Missionary Training Institute." Bible school was meant to prepare students to go forth and save the world.

Alas, I was not cut out for the role in which my education tried to prepare me. Nevertheless, I did try to follow the model and teaching I learned from my Pentecostal mentors. Once I entered the ministry I labored to nurture the spiritual lives of the faithful on Sunday mornings through biblical sermons and win sinners to salvation on Sunday evenings with evangelistic messages. I just never succeeded in making this model work in any of my pastorates in Foursquare churches.

*   *   *   *   *

For all the great professors whose teaching I absorbed and for all the important information I learned in Bible college, I cannot remember learning anything that prepared me for the ministry God gave me twenty years later. The irony of Bible college is it

CHUCK SMITH: A MEMOIR OF GRACE

sometimes leads you all around the Bible without ever taking you into it. I do not think I even read the Bible all the way through until some time after Bible college. Seeing that evangelism was the stated mission of the church, the conversion of sinners took precedence over all other concerns.

I did receive a basic understanding of the Greek and Hebrew languages and how to use the scholarly tools necessary for biblical research. But I wish I had also been taught a well-rounded Bible study method and learned how to discern the message of biblical books, how to break them down according to their internal structure, and how to find the meaning of a passage. I had to learn all this on my own.

Bible college did teach me to turn to God in all situations. This was tested later and proven under unrelenting financial pressure, the overwhelming need of people in my church, sudden emergencies, and heartbreaking losses. Bible college nurtured in us a belief that God is as active today as any other time in human history, that He answers prayer, and that He still heals the sick and rescues us out of all our troubles. Nothing braces a minister for the soul-battering storms that assail him, his family, and his congregation better than the unshakable conviction that God is near and powerful to save.

A few of my professors left a profound impression on my life. I was drawn to those professors who had an intellectual depth. Something about their approach to Scripture and theology really appealed to me. I wanted to hang on to the idea that a person could be both Christian and smart. Regrettably, a few people I had encountered in my Pentecostal upbringing felt that human intelligence was more likely to get in God's way than to glorify Him.

The professors I appreciated most and who exercised the greatest influence in my life and ministry shared the following traits: strong intellect, fierce love for God, and the ability to clearly and passionately communicate the truth of Scripture.

Dr. Nathaniel Van Cleave had come from the University of Southern California to teach at LIFE Bible College. Few speakers were as spellbinding as Dr. Van Cleave. He riveted us to the edge of our seats even as he taught us how to construct and deliver a sermon.

Dr. Luther Myer affected us with his devotion to God as much as he did with his knowledge of Scripture. Listening to Dr. Myer created within us a desire to aspire to a life of intimate devotion to God. Through his classes we discovered not only the miracle-working God of Pentecost, but also the loving Father who invites His children into a day-by-day, moment-by-moment closeness with Him.

Dr. Guy Duffield was an excellent expositor. I could remember his sermons even weeks or months after I heard them because they were so logically prepared and spiritually meaningful.

Just one sentence spoken by one professor had the force to radically change my ministry and put me on a new course after years of struggling in small churches. That professor was Elmer Gottschalk. By the time his words came back to me, I had exhausted every

CHUCK SMITH: A MEMOIR OF GRACE

other resource I had received from Bible college. I cannot even remember what subject Dr. Gottschalk taught. I only remember that in one class he made the statement, "The book of Romans will revolutionize any church that studies its way through it." This sentence returned to me a decade after graduation and pushed me straight into my God-given destiny.

....

[1] The term, "slain in the Spirit" is used among Pentecostal and charismatic Christians to refer to an experience in which God's Spirit comes to rest on people with such force that they cannot remain on their feet, but collapse in a kind of euphoric swoon. Although fainting is a normal human experience, I have always had serious reservations about attributing these particular fainting spells to God.

[2] *The Abolition of Man* by C. S. Lewis, pp. 34-35, Macmillan Publishing Company, NY, 1955.

4

CHAPTER FOUR

Between my junior and senior years of college, I lined up a series of speaking engagements from Omaha, Nebraska to Wheeling, West Virginia. Through my professors, visiting clergy, and other students I had developed contacts with Foursquare ministers in those areas. So I wrote a few letters and created an itinerary. And after my brother, Paul, finished his high school graduation ceremonies, we got into our car and headed east.

I was hoping this stint as "traveling evangelists" would provide us with valuable experience, but even more so that I would begin to get an idea of the sort of ministry God had in mind for me. I am not certain either one of us gained or learned anything useful at the time or that helped later with the churches we served. We did, however, meet some wonderful people who were kind and patient enough to allow us to practice on them in our fledgling attempts at preaching. I pray there is a special dispensation of mercy for young and sincere preachers who mask their nervousness with bravado as they deliver sermons pieced together with ideas gleaned from others.

I learned long ago that I cannot predict the various ways that God's grace will enter our lives. Sometimes an opportunity seemingly falls from the sky. Other times we create our own opportunities and a few of them even work out. Then there are those times when God's grace enters our program or effort and takes us somewhere we would have never been able to go on our own.

From Omaha we journeyed on to Toledo, Ohio. When we arrived, the pastor gave us a quick tour of the city and then introduced us to the chief of police, to let him know we were there and that we would be holding services in the Foursquare church. While discussing our plans, the police chief warned us of a local gang that had been stirring up a lot of trouble. Mostly they had been provoking fights with other gangs, but they also drove around looking for young men to beat up at random. "Watch your back," the chief told us.

One morning while Paul and I walked up the street to the home where we were staying, a car filled with young hoods pulled up suddenly to the curb. The first person to jump out was the leader of the notorious gang that was plaguing the city. Tensing up, we prepared to defend ourselves. "Here we go," I said to Paul.

The leader, however, did not seem menacing at all. Instead, he began a conversation. "Are you the guys from California?" When we said that we were, he asked, "Do you play ball?" Of course we did. He told us, "Well, we have a game this afternoon and we need a couple of players. Do you wanna play?"

My brother and I have always loved sports—and are quite competitive—so we jumped at the chance. Paul was quite a pitcher, so when we took our positions in the field, he pitched while I caught. The team we joined that afternoon was playing a rival gang from the other side of the city—a team against whom they had never been able to win even one game. But by the end of the last inning, Paul had pitched a shut out and we both had hit a couple of home runs. We became instant heroes and the gang's leader lined up as many games as he could while we were still in town.

We organized a beach party at the end of that week on the shores of Lake Eerie in Monroe, Michigan. When it grew dark, we built a big bonfire around which everyone gathered. Before long, the fire drew what seemed like a million June bugs. Some of the young people began to bat the bugs away with their towels to prevent them from flying into the fire. But that only dazed the persistent bugs temporarily, after which they recovered and flew straight into the flames.

The evening's agenda included music provided by the church and a sermon delivered by me. When I began to speak, I had the perfect illustration to accompany my message. "Like those bugs flying into the fire," I explained, "humans are bent on self-destruction through their sinful behavior. In dying for us, Jesus did His best to keep us from diving into hell. Sadly, we either resist His sacrifice or ignore His attempt to rescue us."

The following night we held the closing meeting of our weeklong ministry. The North Side Gang came, completely filling one side of the church. At the end of the service, when people were invited forward to turn their lives over to Jesus, the entire gang—to the very last young man—came forward. When I went to pray with them, it became clear that they really did not understand what was going on. "Do you know about Jesus?" I asked them.

"Not really," was their response.

So I gave them as clear an explanation of salvation as I could. Afterward I asked them, "How come you came forward tonight?"

They answered, "You played ball with us, so we wanted to play ball with you."

* * * * *

After a productive summer, I returned to Bible college and threw myself into my last semester. But once I completed my courses, I still felt uncertain about stepping right into ministry. I did not feel ready to jump into being a senior pastor, but no other opportunities for Christian service had presented themselves to me. I made myself as available to God as I could, but it seemed like I was on the station platform not knowing which train to board.

I decided to take another road trip, this time by myself because Paul was busy with his studies. I contacted a pastor I knew who had moved to Missouri to let him know I was interested in coming out and preaching at youth meetings. He sounded excited on the phone and assured me there was plenty to do, so I began my travel plans and sermon preparation. But when I arrived in town, the church seemed unaware that I was coming. No special meetings had been planned. I received a warm welcome, but the response to my suggestion of holding a youth rally was less than enthusiastic.

After a few days I decided to contact another church in town and offer them my services. I figured that since I had already come all that way, I might as well keep myself busy. Right away the other church agreed to work with me and announced a week of outreach meetings for the young people. By midweek we had a fairly good turnout and I felt better about being there. I was grateful that God was using me in ways I had hoped He would.

By the end of the week, however, problems surfaced. The church I had initially come to work with heard how well the meetings were going and asked me to return on the weekend for a big youth night service they had decided to host. At first it looked like I would be very busy, but soon I discovered that the two churches had become engaged in a contest to see who could draw the most people and I was at the center of their competition.

Now, I've always enjoyed athletic competition and in my prime I never backed down from an opportunity to join a team and pit our skills against a rival. But I have never been comfortable bringing that same spirit of competition into ministry. Perhaps it is because competition creates winners and losers, and that does not fit well into the context of Jesus' ministry in the Gospels. Or maybe it's because in his description of the body of Christ in Romans 12 and 1 Corinthians 12, Paul paints a picture that depicts cooperation rather than competition. At any rate, Paul is clear on the fact that our battles are not supposed to be fought within the church, but against hostile forces outside our spiritual community, "For we wrestle not against flesh and blood" (Ephesians 6:12).

Before these two churches could run me up and down the field or score points against each other, I decided to leave Missouri and return home. I had enjoyed my opportunities to speak and pray with people, but I was somewhat disappointed with the whole experience and felt as unprepared for ministry as ever. I returned to Los Angeles, got a job, and stayed close to the Bible college and its faculty so that if a position opened up for ministry, everyone would know I was available and ready. In the meantime, I stayed active with my friends and some of the students from the college.

Once in a while on Sunday nights, a few of us would attend an African-American church in the Watts neighborhood. We enjoyed the rhythm and energy of their music—a precursor to the rock-n-roll that emerged from African-American gospel music in the south a decade later. When their preacher was on his game (or "under the anointing") he was a force of nature. He not only thundered the gospel, but also maintained an ongoing, unscripted, yet clearly defined conversation with his audience, who urged him on to a higher voltage of inspiration through their own inspired chatter of, "Bless him, Lord!" "Yes, brother, preach it!" and the perfectly-timed, "Amen!"

One Sunday night while sitting in that church in Watts a few minutes before the service, I spotted another student from the Bible college. He was with several other people—one of them a young woman who stood out from the others. *How does he do it?* I wondered. This guy was always surrounded by the loveliest women. I did not want to stare, but I couldn't help but notice that this young lady was especially attractive.

About a week later, my brother, Paul, pitched a ball game for the Bible college. Every week during the regular season his team played other colleges around L.A. County. Because this was a home game, they played on the ball field at Echo Park not far from the campus. Up in the bleachers, waiting for the game to begin, I sat talking casually with the young lady next to me.

A few minutes later, the guy I had seen Sunday night arrived with several other students, including the beautiful young woman who had been with him at church. The row directly in front of me was open, and this guy and his entourage sat down there—all except the really beautiful one. She first turned and with her handkerchief began dusting the bleacher.

"Here!" I announced, "I've already dusted this one for you." Then scooting away from the girl next to me, I made space for Catheryn.

"Thank you," she said with a smile as she sat down next to me.

A few minutes into our conversation, she mentioned that she may have left some books at school that she needed that weekend. "I've got a car," I said, "and I'd be happy to drive you to campus."

Catheryn, or Kay, was unlike any girl I had ever known. Beautiful all the time, glamorous when she dolled herself up, and she also had a depth that I had not encountered with other young women. She was very intelligent and had an insatiable appetite to learn. Her interests went in every conceivable direction: math, science, medicine, psychology, and so on. More than anything, Kay was radically devoted to Jesus Christ. She embraced Him in faith as if her very existence depended on her bond with Him. Wherever He could use her, she wanted to go. Whatever path He chose for her, she wanted to follow.

Six weeks later we were married.

Of course, with such a brief courtship people told us our marriage would never make it. Perhaps they were right. It has only been sixty-two years now since we tied the knot, so who knows if our marriage will stand the test of time! But I do have to say this: I love my wife today more than ever before, more than I love anyone, and more than I ever knew I could love another human.

Having graduated from Bible college, cut my teeth as a traveling evangelist, and found myself a bride who was willing to go with me to the ends of the earth, I was now ready to step into the Lord's work and begin my career in pastoring a church.

* * * * *

Kay's family had lived in L.A. and attended services at Angelus Temple for many years. At one time Kay had played the clarinet in the temple orchestra. Later, however, her parents purchased property in Hemet, California where they could stable horses and soon they were spending their weekends away from the city—and away from church.

Kay had an older sister whose name was Louise Webster, but we always addressed her by her nickname, EC. Since EC had dedicated her life to Christian service, she noticed Kay was beginning to drift in her spiritual life and felt concerned for her future. So EC told their parents that Kay had confided in her that her deepest desire was to attend Bible college. Soon Kay was enrolled at LIFE and she determined never again to allow any distance to grow between her and God.

EC had moved to Phoenix, Arizona in the 1930s and founded the First Foursquare Church of Phoenix, where she continued to serve for more than thirty-five years. She became the director of Foursquare churches for that region, which included all of Arizona. She also became the spiritual leader of a cadre of dedicated men and women who planted and served in churches that drew most of their members from poor communities or provided Christian and humanitarian aid on the reservations of Native Americans.

A few weeks after our wedding, Kay and I packed our few possessions and moved to Prescott, Arizona where EC had arranged for me to assume the pastorate in the small Foursquare church planted there. The few people who attended the church were hardworking and well-meaning, but they could only provide fifteen dollars a week for our income. Kay's parents helped us out with a weekly check, so we were able to get by, but barely. Needless to say, we never had spare change in our pockets—but we never missed a meal either.

Poverty offers important lessons if one is willing to pay attention. Sometimes it's due to low income, but a great deal of poverty is the

CHUCK SMITH: A MEMOIR OF GRACE

result of poor spending habits, living above one's means, purchasing consumables, and making poor or risky investments. We found that when we lived on pennies, we had to make the most of each one. I think the psalmist must have had the poor in mind when he said, "Trust not in oppression, and become not vain in robbery: if riches increase, set not your heart upon them" (Psalm 62:10). The way out of poverty does not include abuse or theft. If we saw an increase in our income, we tried not to think about it and continued to live frugally, paying close attention to each dime we spent.

During that time, God taught us how to survive on a meager income. He was also teaching us the enjoyment of life's free pleasures and the fact that we did not "live on bread only, but by every word that proceeds out of the mouth of the LORD" (Deuteronomy 8:3 NKJV). Later in life I learned that many ministers had gotten themselves into trouble—and not only spiritual trouble. Some even landed themselves in prison because they had mishandled their church's finances. So God taught us important lessons regarding our finances and showed Kay and me that a good life did not depend on money. Those lessons seemed trivial when we were scraping the bottom of our dresser drawers for stray coins, but learning to handle money with wisdom and integrity played a vital role in the ministry God brought us into many years later. Through those hard times we learned that "He that is faithful in that which is least is faithful also in much: and he that is unjust in the least is unjust also in much" (Luke 16:10).

We went into the ministry for God, so whether or not our salary was sufficient for our means was irrelevant. For about the first twenty years of our ministry, Kay and I took side jobs to pay the bills and keep the family clothed and fed. We were determined to "make the gospel of Christ without charge" and not abuse our position in any way (1 Corinthians 9:18). We never went to anyone in the church for a handout or a loan and we kept our needs to ourselves—although at times it may have been obvious to others that we were struggling. We also tried to model trust in God for our children, so we never complained about money matters but took every need to God in prayer.

After less than a year in Prescott, Arizona Kay became pregnant with our first child, Janette. Both Kay and I wanted to return to our families in California, because the medical care we could afford in Prescott was substandard compared to what was available back home. We loved the folks we had served that first year of our marriage, but neither Kay nor I felt that was where God intended us to put down roots. We were Californians at heart.

Nevertheless, not long after Jan was born another opportunity to pastor a church opened for us in Tucson, Arizona. So once again we packed the car and took the long, hot drive through the desert to a small church in a burgeoning community.

*   *   *   *   *

Our two-and-a-half years in Tucson turned out to be a delightful experience. Being a young couple, we tended to attract other young couples so there was this sense of vibrancy and expectation in our church community. The older members who attended before we arrived greeted us with open arms and warm hearts. They also enjoyed the influx of young people and were willing mentors who provided all of us a great deal of encouragement and support.

The Tucson church was better off financially than Prescott and it could afford to pay a salary of twenty-five dollars a week. They also provided us a parsonage, which was actually a room behind the sanctuary. A water spigot from an outside pipe came through a wall in an area we called "the kitchen." We had a large metal tub under the spigot, but we would have to heat the water over the stove before using it for washing dishes or bathing the babies—Chuck jr. was born during our pastorate there. I was able to create two rooms by building a divider between "the kitchen" and "the other room" that served as a bookcase on one side and shelves for our pots, pans, and dishes on the other. We used the restrooms located near the entrance of the church, and members who lived down the street allowed Kay and me to bathe in their home.

We were blessed by one family in the church that spent summers in their home in Minnesota, but who were affluent enough to maintain a home all year round in Tucson. While away, they allowed us to stay in their home, which was a great luxury for us beyond our dreams. We have never forgotten their kindness.

My web of friends and relationships was about to weave another interesting pattern in the design of God's ongoing preparation of my future calling. To appreciate the re-connection at this particular intersection requires a flashback to my Camp Radford days.

One of the friendships I struck up at Camp Radford began on the baseball diamond. Glen York had come to camp with his church's youth group, which had enough players to field a complete baseball team, except for one position. When I heard they did not have a pitcher, I volunteered. Glen was the catcher, so naturally we got to know each other pretty well in a short period of time. We did not see each other much after that week at camp, but I never forgot Glen and he never forgot me.

Little did I know, but Glen happened to be stationed at Davis-Monthan Air Force Base, which is not far from Tucson. One Sunday, a few months after we had moved to Tucson, Glen set out to find a Foursquare church in town where he could worship. That is when he walked into the back door of our church—or the front door of our home, depending on your point of view.

Glen became like a member of our family and his friendship continually renewed our spirits through the challenges of an expanding, yet financially feeble ministry. Glen would be one more piece of the puzzle in our lives, although the puzzle itself was a long way from being complete or even clearly defined.

After two-and-a-half years in Tucson, a pastoral position became available at a church in Corona, California. Eager to return to our native state and live less than thirty miles from my folks, Kay and I jumped at the opportunity. Another reason why I was pleased (and relieved) to receive the invitation to move to Corona had to do with a concern that had been growing in my heart during our last few months in Arizona. By piecing together everything I had learned at Bible college, I had developed a repertory of exactly two-and-a-half years' worth of sermons. As I approached the end of my collection of messages, I began to wonder what I would do when I ran out of sermons. The invitation to Corona was a reprieve. I could start from the beginning and have another two-and-a-half more years' worth of sermons again—or so I thought.

At the time we had moved to Tucson, the city was in a state of rapid growth and development. Many people from the southern and eastern states came to the Arizona deserts for relief from various respiratory ailments. The community was young and mobile and the church was willing to take a risk with a young man with new ideas. Corona, on the other hand, was an old city that had not seen much development. The people in our church were Foursquare and wanted to remain Foursquare, which meant they were looking for a preacher who was everything that made me feel uncomfortable.

These social dynamics were not apparent to us at first. Leaving behind a thriving ministry in Tucson that had grown under my pastorate, I arrived in Corona with all the confidence of a young man who is very sure of himself. In fact, I came to Corona with a false confidence based on our recent success. *I know how to do this*, I thought. *It makes no difference where I go, because I can build a dynamic ministry anywhere.* Corona, however, taught me that I could not do it. Our first Sunday in town, fifty-two people attended the service. Our last Sunday only twenty-seven people came to church, and six of those people were family members, including Mom, Dad, and my brother, Bill.

We did find one ray of hope within our church. Mrs. Ezell was a wonderful woman who loved God and was devoted to prayer.

Her son, John, was about our same age, and he and his wife, Velma, reminded us of the kind of dynamic young Christians we had befriended in Tucson. I kept thinking that if we could attract couples like John and Velma to our church, we could get it off the ground and flourishing. John and Velma, however, were already committed to and involved in another local church. We never saw the fulfillment of our wishes—at least not at that time.

We gave it our best shot in Corona. In order to minister there and still pay our bills, I took a full-time job in a local grocery store. But nothing came easy in this season of our lives. We suffered through a few personal mishaps—a couple of unexpected trips to the emergency room and a small fire in our home—and in those instances, the people in the church were kind to us. But they never really took to us. We wanted desperately to win their approval and support, but we were losing that battle.

I want to again emphasize the fact that financial hardship traveled with us for many years. For the very reason that money was scarce, we had to continue to learn to trust God. During these tight years, He taught us invaluable lessons about putting our faith in His faithfulness and watching Him come through for us. He did so—every single time.

We also learned something about God's timing. God rarely took action within the time frame that we wished for, yet we never went without a meal. We learned through the lean years that God has resources we know nothing about. We couldn't have predicted the creative ways in which He met our needs, nor could we have predicted the ways in which God would magnify those lessons. Learning to trust Him for five dollars so we could buy groceries and put dinner on the table was, in fact, preparation for the trust we would need in the next step in ministry, when the need wouldn't be five dollars, but millions of dollars. We learned that money is not the greatest or most important factor in doing God's work. I don't believe it even belongs in the list of the top ten factors.

God knew what He had in mind for the future and He was preparing us. He was preparing me in particular, because I would eventually face challenges with church boards when I asked them to set money issues to one side for the sake of God's will.

When we arrived in Corona we moved into a small home that needed a few repairs. I broke out my tool belt and Kay performed her magic by decorating the interior on a zero-based budget. One day when the owner came by to collect the rent, she noticed the improvements. Within a week she served us an eviction notice because she wanted to move back into her refurbished home. At the time, Kay was pregnant with our third child, Jeffrey.

The landlady kept calling to remind me, "You must be out by the first." I would calmly reassure her, "We will be out by then and you will be able to move in on the first."

She would then ask, "Have you found a place yet?"

"No," I answered honestly.

"Well, you have to be out."

"Yes, I know, Ma'am, and I assure you that we will be out."

Our budget for monthly rent was limited and inflexible. There were not many homes in Corona at that time which fell into our price range. But each time the landlady called to quiz me on whether we had found a new place, I explained that even though nothing had come up yet, we would certainly be out by the first. Perhaps somewhere in the back of her mind she felt a twinge of guilt for turning a young family out on the street. But judging by her telephone presence I could not say that with any certainty.

The night before we were supposed to be out, she called once more and asked, "Have you found a place yet?"

When I told her no she became livid and began screaming into the phone. I said, "Ma'am, we're moving out tomorrow just as I have promised."

A family in the church was kind enough to let us store our furniture in their garage. In the meantime, I took my pregnant wife and two children down to Santa Ana where I thought we would live with my folks until something opened up for us. That wasn't the best arrangement, but we were prepared to do whatever it would take to continue our service to the church in Corona.

The very Saturday evening we went to live with my folks, the phone rang while we were eating dinner. The people in whose garage we had stored our furniture called with some good news. A moving van had pulled up to the house next to theirs and they learned from the owners that the family that had been renting it was moving out. They did not, as yet, have any lead on new renters. Not only that, but the monthly rent was within our budget.

How's that for timing? God waited until the very day we had to move before He provided our new home. God wanted to show us He knows our needs and is in control. This was yet another reminder and guarantee that we could trust Him in all things. Though I was failing in the church, I was still learning about the faithfulness of God.

*   *   *   *   *

When Kay's mom passed away, I asked the store manager for time off to attend the funeral and to spend time with Kay's sister, EC.

"No problem," the manager assured me. I knew that he liked me and appreciated my work. In fact, vice presidents from the regional offices had offered me management positions, which were quite tempting in light of my dismal experience with the church. But I turned them down each time because a career in management would have taken me from the work to which I had been called.

When we returned from Phoenix, I drove by the store to check my hours for the coming week. When I did not find my name on the schedule, I went to the manager to find out if there had been some oversight. He apologetically informed me that while I was gone, someone from union headquarters called to let him know that my dues were late. I would not be allowed to return to work until I paid my delinquent dues. When I went to the union offices to bring my dues up to date, they assessed me a late-payment fine. I explained the death in the family but they were adamant. Until my dues and my fine were paid in full, I could not return to work in the store. Of course, we simply did not have the extra money and there was no way to come up with any cash without work.

Turning to leave the union offices, the last ounce of hope drained from my heart. We had come to Corona full of bright dreams and enthusiasm, but all of that had been knocked out of me. Corona had become a disaster. In all my life I had never given up on anything. If I set out on a job or project, I always saw it through to the end. Quitting was simply not in my profile or character. But we had failed in our church, despite doing everything we knew to do, everything we had been trained to do. And now I couldn't even hold a regular job.

With slumped shoulders and my head hanging down, I resigned from the church and gave up on the ministry. I would move back to Santa Ana and take any sort of job I could find until I found a new career to pursue. I had attempted to do the work to which I believed God had called me, but it ended—not with a crash, but a whimper. Now it was time to cut my losses and find a real job.

Of course, the only piece to the puzzle visible to me was that particular moment in time. God's plan for the radical revelation He was to give me, the new direction He was to take my ministry, and the profound confirmation He would send me was hidden in the future. All I knew then and there was bitter disappointment, failure, and heartache.

I understand now that it can be good to sit in failure and come to the end of yourself. Through broken dreams and shattered plans one learns humility and total dependence on God. If I knew then what I know now, I would have whistled joyfully as we drove from Corona. By steps—and rather gentle steps, all things considered—

God took me out of a situation where I would never be able to do my best work and into a harvest field vaster than my imagination.

I didn't know it at the time, but I see now that the receiving of my ordination after Bible college created an illusion within me. I assumed that with my education complete, I was prepared for ministry. But the truth is, the years between my twenty-first birthday and my thirty-eighth were an ongoing education in God's classroom. In fact, I have not yet left His class, although now I find it a greater joy to be there than earlier in my life. If God had told me on our way to Prescott that I would spend the next seventeen years in His school, I might have given up in frustration right then and there. It would be a few years before I came across the passage in Zechariah where God asks, "For who has despised the day of small things?" (Zechariah 4:10), but I was learning its meaning through my real-life experiences.

Back in Santa Ana, I landed a job driving a delivery truck for a uniform company. Although my thoughts kept telling me, *I failed at ministry*, a persistent sense of my calling kept nagging at me. I had attempted a work for the Lord, but in the next phase of my life I would learn that "we are His workmanship, created in Christ Jesus unto good works, which God has before ordained that we should walk in them" (Ephesians 2:10).

5

CHAPTER FIVE

"THE PREACHER HAS THE HIGHEST OF CALLINGS and the noblest of arts. His work is done to alter the human will and transform the character, which he does not accomplish, of course, without the aid of God's Spirit; but as God's partner, the preacher's task is worthy of all the cultivation and perfection which it can be given.... If my preaching has only an infinitesimal part to play in the results which follow, I will believe that the Master wants me to do that part with the greatest skill possible; only let me give the Master all the glory, for 'I am what I am by the grace of God.'"

Handbook of Preaching by Dr. Nathaniel M. Van Cleave [1]

Start the engine, accelerate, turn the steering wheel, and brake. Take Fourth Street to Main then turn left. Every week I followed the same route with a delivery truck until it seemed more like a habit than a job. I did not intend to make a career of delivering clean uniforms, but it was a way to earn money during our transition. The monotonous pattern of my regular rounds gave me a lot of time to think about the future. I took an inventory of my life experience, dreams, education, and skills I had acquired and weighed them against the responsibility I carried for my family. I tried to envision myself in several different occupations, but none were compelling to me nor could I imagine feeling fulfilled in a career I landed in by choice rather than by calling. I had loved being in ministry and perhaps the grief of losing that opportunity clouded my vision so that nothing else seemed appealing or even interesting.

Although it felt as if I had been driving that delivery truck for years, it had actually been less than three months. During this time, I was having dinner at my folks' house when the phone rang and the caller wanted to speak with me. When I picked up the receiver, Dr. Van Cleave was on the other end of the line.

"Nate" Van Cleave who I mentioned earlier, had been one of my heroes in Bible college. For some reason, he had taken an interest in Kay and me and had followed our progress in ministry from a distance. Not long after I graduated, Dr. Van Cleave moved to Santa Ana to serve as the Orange County district supervisor for the Foursquare Church. Unbeknown to me, when he learned that I had resigned in Corona and left ministry, he began to look for a church that would be a good fit for us. Although I had failed the church in Corona, Van Cleave did not lose faith in me. He knew that the road to successful service for God is lined with failure. Until we come to the end of ourselves, we cannot learn the fullness of what God desires to do through our lives.

Dr. Van Cleave told me about a church that was looking for a new pastor and asked me to apply as a candidate for the position. If I was willing to give it a try, he would arrange for me to preach there one Sunday. My heart was ready for this call. It took very little deliberation for me to realize that God was giving me a second chance. When I told Dr. Van Cleave I would give it a shot, he began telling me about this church in Huntington Beach—a church less than twenty minutes from my parents' home in Santa Ana.

Kay and I immediately fell in love with the church and the people were equally openhearted toward us. Huntington Beach in the mid-1950s was like the coastal community of Ventura where I had grown up, so in some ways it felt like coming home. We quickly made friends, both in the church and in the community, and settled in to the best experience in ministry we had ever known.

Those wonderful years in Huntington Beach would require several volumes rather than one chapter. Our children were growing up and as each of them turned five, they began their education in the Huntington Beach elementary school, took swim classes in the summer, learned to ride a bike, and so on. My parents regularly attended the church and were always nearby when needed. My dad and brother, Bill, helped me build a room addition to the parsonage next door to the church. I think Kay and I could have easily stayed in that church and community for the rest of our lives.

We were blessed with a good percentage of church members around our same age. After we arrived and plunged into the ministry, other families with young children began to attend. A good number of young people also became active in the church. Many of these teenagers came from homes without religious commitment or training. But these kids were finding life in Jesus and the energy of their love for God drew others like themselves.

We also had a contingent of older men and women who remembered the glory days of the Foursquare Church. But unlike the church in Corona, they did not insist on rolling back the clock or freezing time. They rejoiced to see the church rejuvenated with the addition of younger members. To our advantage, the devout elderly provided the ministry with a much-needed undergirding of prayer. In fact, those prayers of the senior women and men have always been the backbone of our ministries. Their insistence that the ongoing work of the Holy Spirit would always be central to the life of the church helped to keep the ministry spiritually vibrant without becoming excessively emotional or demonstrative.

All in all, we had stepped into a situation that was as ideal as anything we could have imagined. The church's growth since we arrived had been observable, but not remarkable. We were content with what God was doing and I kept busy with sermon preparation, visitation, youth activities, and the hundreds of little things a pastor does that no one notices. Kay stepped in wherever help was needed—teaching Sunday school, assisting with worship and organizing various events. Of course, I still had to take odd jobs now and then to keep us afloat, and Kay also filled in a variety of roles for the Foursquare denomination, both in their headquarters and in local offices. Her excellent office skills included shorthand, typing, and flawless grammar and spelling. It seemed as though this small church ministry was perfectly suited to us and everything moved smoothly.

Nevertheless, something was missing. When that "something" finally surfaced, it caused the work of God in our lives to take another major turn. We had no idea our ministry was incomplete, and if it had been brought to our attention, I don't think we could have guessed what was lacking. Even still, as we approached our second year in Huntington Beach, I could see dark clouds forming on the horizon. Despite the fact that the church was running along well and our whole family was enjoying steady and healthy growth, I felt an undeniable, unexplainable pinch of anxiety.

* * * * *

In the Foursquare denomination headquarters, leaders made strategic decisions regarding churches that were growing, had leveled out, or were in decline. So it wasn't unusual for a minister to be transferred from one church to another every few years. Hoping to find a "good match," our supervisors would evaluate a pastor's strengths and a church's needs. Ministers and their families were liable to move to a new church if it looked like they would be more successful with another congregation or if a particular church needed their specific talents.

At first this nomadic life in ministry worked in my favor. That's because I had enough material to produce two years' worth of sermons. If I served the same church for more than two years, I would have to start repeating my sermons. I might be able to get away with it for a while without anyone noticing, but my own heart would berate me for compromising my integrity.

The dilemma I faced was the fact that we had landed in a wonderful position. As the psalmist said, "The lines have fallen to me in pleasant places; yes, I have a good inheritance" (Psalm 16:6 NKJV). We were happy in Huntington Beach and did not want to move, but I was running out of sermons and that created a potential crisis that needed resolving. Five decades later, having developed a greater understanding of the breadth and depth of the Bible, it seems comical that I would ever worry about running out of sermons to preach. But my predicament at that time points out the inadequacy of the training I received for ongoing ministry and of a personal renewal in God's Word.

In the course of my biblical studies I had picked up *The Apostle John* by W. H. Griffith Thomas.[2] I began reading this book at the same time I was worrying about my diminishing supply of sermons. In his study of John's life, Dr. Thomas included outline studies of the epistle of 1 John. For some reason, those outlines really gripped me. Until then, the practice of preaching I followed was what I had seen and heard growing up in church and in my Bible college days. A preacher would select a random text from the Bible, maybe give some information about its context (and maybe not), and then develop a message based on what could be seen in one verse or short passage. The central theme of the sermon would be centered on a topic such as, salvation, repentance, faith—rather than a development of the theme that lay behind the biblical text. I quoted a lot of other verses, and in that sense my sermons were doctrinally sound, but they did not bring us any closer to what the Bible actually said in the text I used for my sermon.

Dr. Thomas, however, had carefully studied and analyzed the entire book of 1 John, noted distinctive features of the book, and developed outlines that not only explored the depths of this remarkable document, but also offered useful application to the Christian's everyday life. It suddenly occurred to me that I could use his outlines of 1 John as the basis of a series of sermons and have enough material to continue preaching for at least another year. So that is what I began to do in our third year in Huntington Beach.

I can't take credit for having predicted what would happen when I preached through 1 John. Unlike other ministers, I never have been one to create a "five-year plan" for any of my churches. I am not the kind of person to dream up, implement, and then manage a strategic program and achieve a successful conclusion. So when our church had experienced significant growth by the end of the third year, I was as surprised as anyone.

Not only had the church grown (the attendance literally doubled), but the people had also grown stronger in their relationship with God and deeper in their love and faith. They had also become more joyful. As I considered their new attitude, it occurred to me that John had this very objective in mind when he wrote his epistle, "And these things we write unto you, that your joy may be full" (1 John 1:4). Their joy was the harvest of what God's Word had planted in their hearts.

We saw more people come to faith and more baptisms that year than in both previous years put together. People were being brought to Jesus, not through my sermons—I was not preaching evangelistic messages—but through the lives of our church members.

The book of Hebrews was probably written to a second generation of Christians and recognized that believers' spiritual lives were in danger of stagnating if they remained in the shallow end of the pool. They had been in the faith long enough that they could have become teachers by now, but sadly they were still infants. So the writer encouraged them to leave aside "the principles of the doctrine of Christ;" that is, reviewing the basics over and over again and "go on unto perfection" or maturity (Hebrews 6:1). Until I began to teach 1 John, I had failed the congregation in this very thing. I had not taken them into maturity with my topical, evangelistic sermons. Over time I have come to see and experience the truth and value of what Paul meant when he said that God gave the church gifted leaders, including "pastors and teachers; for the perfecting of the saints, for the work of the ministry, for the edifying of the body of Christ" (Ephesians 4:11-13).

I did not immediately make the connection between my teaching through a book in the Bible and all the positive results that followed. Without knowing it, I had stumbled on a real need in the hearts of many believers. Thousands of Christians attended church but I felt they weren't learning anything. They owned Bibles, but reading through the Bible was a frustrating experience for them. It was similar to the Ethiopian eunuch reading the scroll of Isaiah. When Philip asked whether he understood what he was reading, the eunuch responded, "How can I, except some man should guide me?" (Acts 8:31). People wanted to know the Bible, but they needed a guide.

*   *   *   *   *

Over the next few years, God developed and refined my calling and service to His people. I was someone who had the privilege of learning about God and the Bible at the feet of a few really great thinkers. Not being an intellectual myself, there wasn't a danger that I would evolve into a seminarian. But standing between the intellectual giants and the average believer, I was able to translate the richness and depth of Scripture into ordinary language. Or to explain my role in a visual image, God permitted me to stand on a ladder and reach to some of the higher shelves to pull down items for people standing on the floor.

Of course, teaching through Griffith Thomas' outline of 1 John had an endpoint, so I had to seek another source of sermon material when we concluded that series. I discovered that taking the congregation through a biblical book gave me plenty of sermon material. It got them excited about studying the Bible and they started asking a lot of questions. We seemed to be on a roll so I decided the best thing I could do was choose another book and preach on it from beginning to end. But which of the sixty-five remaining books would I tackle next? I was pretty sure it wouldn't be Leviticus. Which one would be the best for us to journey through—and how would I choose?

That is when Professor Gottschalk's statement from Bible college came back to mind: "The book of Romans will revolutionize any church that studies through it." *Of course, the book of Romans!* This was the central document of Christian theology—the book that launched Martin Luther's Protestant Reformation, warmed the heart of John Wesley, and made the case for the doctrine of "justification by faith." I suppose it was rather naive to think I could

CHUCK SMITH: A MEMOIR OF GRACE

take on this grand and profound epistle with less than a decade of ministry under my belt. Nevertheless, Romans turned out to be an important challenge in my post-graduate education and a personal revelation that transformed my relationship with God, my view of myself, and my ministry to God's people.

While studying William Newell's commentary on Romans, I came across an excursus on grace.[3] Now, understand that I had grown up with a works-and-reward model of the Christian life. Whether this is what I had been taught, or I just came up with it myself, it was implicit in my understanding of how we lived in relationship with God. I struggled under the impression that God's love for me was conditional. If I believed God was generous with His blessings, I was also convinced that a person had to be good enough to earn those blessings. For my part, I seldom felt worthy enough to reach the standard set before me in the holiness tradition that preceded Pentecostalism. Therefore, I did not have high expectations that I would ever deserve God's blessing on my life and work.

Newell's development of the nature of God's grace radically changed my thinking. Up until that moment, nothing I had ever learned went so quickly and deeply into the marrow of my being. If God's blessings seemed absent from my life, it was not because I failed to give enough time to my daily devotions, to go door-to-door with the gospel on a weekly basis, or to bring enough sincerity into my worship. Any lack of blessing was—plain and simple—a consequence of not believing it was in God's heart to bless me apart from any merit I could muster.

Newell repeatedly stressed the fact that grace has no cause or reason for the person who receives it. I realized grace was God's blessing when I did not deserve it—to rejoice in His favor at all times, and to be absolutely certain that grace would guide and support me in the future. I cannot say why, but my heart fully embraced the reality of God's grace and ever since I first read these words I have believed that God would give me a blessing every day. To this day, He has not disappointed me.

* * * * *

Without a doubt, I am a blessed man and have enjoyed a wonderful life. I give thanks to God each day for His goodness, and for the fact that He has used me for the spiritual development of His people, church, and kingdom. But it was around the time that I reached for the book of Romans and our church moved into high gear that the greatest single tragedy of my life struck.

Turning back the pages to when we lived in Tucson, Kay's dad had passed away about six weeks before Chuck jr. was born. Although I understood what her dad meant to her, I could not feel the loss as deeply as it gripped Kay's soul. Two years before her father's death, Kay's mother had suffered a stroke. And when her father died, her mother had to move to Phoenix to live with Kay's sister, EC, until she too passed away. Kay, who had been adopted by her parents at birth, was now truly orphaned in the world. But both my parents were still in good health and doing well. Until now, I had been shielded from that agonizing grief of losing someone as close to me as a mother or father.

I am not going to share details of the tragedy that broke over my family like a flood. Those things are personal and would not help you understand the most meaningful aspects of God's work in my life. Instead, I will simply report that an exceptionally dark windstorm howled through Southern California one night, and those contrary winds brought down a single-engine aircraft over Camp Pendleton, snuffing the lives of its pilot and passenger—my youngest brother, Bill, and my dad.

Before the sun rose on Sunday morning, I received word that their crumpled plane had been discovered and there were no survivors. A few hours later I stood in the pulpit with the Book of books open before me and spoke from it the everlasting truth that transcends life and death. The next day I was asked to identify my father's and brother's bodies, and that weekend the chapel at Blower Mortuary was crowded with people who knew and loved Dad and Bill.

I share this with you in order to clarify the reality of God's grace. Yes, there is a divine blessing hidden in every day, free for the taking and totally unrelated to moral cause and effect. But grace does not shield the cruel realities of a world damaged by the fall. We are not in heaven yet and God does not spare us from the crushing blows that come to everyone. We lose people we love. We suffer, we grieve, and we journey on. But even in the darkest nights when awakened by windows shuddering with the blast of a storm, we are not abandoned. Through the wind and over the turbulent sea, grace comes to us with the comfort of heaven, the support of God's Spirit, and the strength to draw our next breath and take the next step. Grace brings hope. Hope pushes forward.

This is all I care to say about that episode and its impact on Mom, my sister, Virginia, my brother, Paul, and myself. Anyone who has listened carefully to my sermons will recognize that all I have ever preached was delivered under the shadow of the cross, which covers and embraces the deepest sorrows and suffering that has reached the human heart. We are children of God's blessings, yes. Even so, we are no strangers to pain.

*   *   *   *   *

Preaching through Romans opened my eyes to the importance of providing people with an authentic knowledge of the Bible. Rather than skip around the Bible from one text to another each Sunday, working straight through a book and presenting each passage in its own context provides believers with the necessary background to read and study the Bible on their own. One of the beautiful by-products of presenting the Bible in this way is the hunger it creates in the hearers. They want to learn more. People began to ask me about resources and references for further study in the Scriptures as they sought to deepen their understanding of God's Word.

Something else happened during our trek through Romans. The shift was so subtle at first that I wasn't even aware it had happened. Later, however, I realized my presentation of God's Word had undergone a significant transformation. The style of speech communication I picked up from preachers in my youth and that my professors modeled in Bible college was enthusiastic, intense, and usually loud. Their preaching, in fact, was a form of oratory widely used in public speeches until the 1970s when television brought the face of the speaker up close to the viewer and a more

CHUCK SMITH: A MEMOIR OF GRACE

conversational style became the norm. Until then, public speakers looked and sounded very much like gospel preachers, as seen in the newsreels of speeches by politicians such as Grover Cleveland, Franklin Roosevelt (e.g. "Day of Infamy"), and John F. Kennedy, who even "pounded the pulpit" in his 1961 inaugural address.

Simply stated, from the beginning of my ministry I had preached topical sermons, but by the time I finished the book of Romans I shifted to the expository teaching of the Bible. The transformation contained three parts: I went from preaching to teaching; the sermon went from topical to expository; and the content of the message went from my own development of a Bible text to the Bible itself.

To appreciate these important changes, I will briefly explain the meaning of these terms.

In the New Testament, preaching was used to make public announcements, so the same Greek word can be translated both as "preach" and "proclaim." The objective of preaching is to motivate people to action. For example, "In those days came John the Baptist, preaching in the wilderness of Judea, and saying, Repent: for the kingdom of heaven is at hand" (Matthew 3:1-2). John's preaching was meant to motivate the people to repent. Preaching attempts to inspire, convict and excite through exhortation, warning, and promise. Teaching differs from preaching in that its objective is to interpret, inform, instruct, explain, clarify, and make application.

According to Dr. Van Cleave, topical sermons "take from the text only a topic or subject. The divisions are invented by the preacher in accordance with the rhetorical possibilities of the subject and the preacher's knowledge of the subject as it is treated in the whole Bible." From the time I graduated Bible college to our first years in Huntington Beach, I built my sermons on one or two Bible verses. But when I began teaching through 1 John, I no longer addressed topics. Instead, I explained the Scriptures. This is expository teaching, which means to examine and develop the meaning of a biblical text. You can get a good idea of what expository teaching looks like from Nehemiah 8:8 (NKJV) where the Levites "read distinctly from the book, in the Law of God; and they *helped them* to understand the reading." The objective of this form of teaching is to put the meaning of Scripture into the hands of the hearers as clearly and simply as possible.

So instead of using verses from the Bible to preach my own (educated) ideas about God and Christian living, I let Scripture speak for itself. As I made these changes—or perhaps I should say that teaching through Romans made these changes in me—people became more interested in the Bible. They were no longer just people in the audience—they were now students or disciples of God's Word. As for me, I realized that I was more comfortable in the role of a teacher and that it suited my personality better than trying to be a preacher.

As a consequence of applying myself to teaching, my library grew rapidly. More than ever before, I found myself needing to turn to reference works and commentaries to get to the heart of a passage or to test my own interpretation against that of biblical scholars. I also collected several works that provided a general survey of the whole Bible, and of those, perhaps my favorite was *Halley's Bible Handbook.* This little resource had been so helpful to me that whenever a member of my church showed an interest in becoming a student of Scripture, it was the first work I recommended. I so often gave my own copy to someone else that I constantly needed to replace it.

Once, after giving away yet one more handbook, I discovered that the publisher had released a new edition. Finding the new copy, I read an endorsement on the jacket that said the most important page in the book was 814. I turned to that page and read, "Each church should have a method of systematically encouraging the congregation to read through the whole Bible."[4] God prepared me for this moment. If I had not already discovered the spiritual value of studying the Scriptures, I might not have taken these words to heart. But having witnessed the way God worked in our lives through 1 John and Romans, I was ready to move further into biblical study.

Up until the moment I read Halley's quote, I cannot remember having read the whole Bible all the way through. It now seems odd to me that in spite of the early training in the Bible, a lifetime spent in church, a fairly early conversion, years of active service, and graduating Bible college, I had never read the Bible straight through. I am not even sure I ever recognized the importance of doing so. Therefore, Halley's suggestion was somewhat of an epiphany to me. Furthermore, he went on to say that ideally "the pastor's Sunday morning sermon would come out of the area that they had been reading the previous week."[5]

From that fairly simple observation came an innovation in the way we structured the church's weekly schedule—one I have adhered to ever since. I decided to do the following:

1. Move our adult Sunday school class to Sunday night. Previously, we held Sunday school classes for all members of the church prior to our regular Sunday morning worship service.

2. Teach a survey of the whole Bible, from Genesis to Revelation, at the pace of five-ten chapters a week.

3. Encourage every church member to read those chapters in preparation for the Sunday evening study.

4. Draw the text for the Sunday morning sermon from somewhere within the same ten chapters.

Studying through the whole Bible is invaluable. The Old Testament provides a necessary foundation for understanding the life, teaching, death and resurrection of Jesus Christ. Making sense of any of the New Testament books requires the Old Testament background—and the book of Hebrews is inaccessible apart from knowledge of Israel's history and religion. The Bible consists of a number of interlinked and interlocked parts. Taken separately, people will naturally misinterpret what they read. But taken together, one part will explain another and altogether the parts explain the whole.

Think of a jigsaw puzzle. If you study just one piece without any idea of what the complete picture looks like, you will never be able to make sense of it. Looking at the whole picture, however, you can see where the one piece fits. By itself, the book of Leviticus is a rather odd document, even a little quirky. But when read as one of the books of Mosaic law from Israel's wilderness period, its message and meaning becomes much clearer. The further back you step away to see the whole picture, the greater your clarity becomes when you investigate the individual pieces.

Going through the entire Bible every two years provided the people in our church with an overview that helped them make sense of each book. Personally, once I embarked on our first journey through the Bible, I stopped worrying about running out of sermon material. With the whole Scripture before us, we could go through the Bible again and again, finding new insights and developing a better knowledge with each trek. I could continue this program of teaching through the Bible on Sunday nights while preaching on texts drawn from our reading on Sunday mornings for the rest of my life. And I have.

*   *   *   *   *

Take one moment or one season of your life, analyze it, and from that experience determine the meaning of your life. You cannot do it. Discrete experiences in life do not carry their own meaning—they do not contain the DNA of the whole. Some Christians make the mistake of getting lost in the moment, of misinterpreting their circumstances, of evaluating whether or not God loves them based on an immediate situation.

Like the Bible, you cannot understand the purpose or value of your life based on one experience or event. Separate the moments of your life—the good and bad, the success and failure, the gains and losses—from the whole, and they make no sense. Interpreting one moment in isolation of every other moment is like trying to understand Leviticus without knowing anything about Exodus, Numbers or Deuteronomy. The parts have to be seen in light of the whole.

Of course, no one can see to the end of their life, which means we cannot interpret momentary events by looking directly at our lives from start to finish. Instead, we need to draw our vision of the whole from the Bible, which gives us a complete picture of what God has in mind for each of us. In one moment, my circumstances may drive me to cry, "O Lord, why have You hidden Your face from me?" but the next moment may bring news that causes me to shout, "I will praise Your name and rejoice in Your goodness forever and ever!" I cannot always discern God's love for me by trying to find it in my circumstances. I learn from the Scriptures that He loves me and then I can interpret my circumstances in the light of that divine love.

For this reason, let me quickly flash back to Tucson and the support and encouragement Kay and I received through Glen York, my friend from summer camp. Even if we had never seen Glen again after we left Arizona, we would have been grateful that God stationed him at the Air Force base near the church where God "stationed" us. If anyone had asked me, "Why do you suppose God intended for you to make friends with Glen York while playing baseball at Camp Radford?" I would have answered, "So that through our renewed friendship in Tucson, Kay and I would have valuable emotional and spiritual support to keep our hearts strong."

I would have been partially right, but significantly wrong.

One Sunday morning, Glen showed up in our church in Huntington Beach. During the years since we'd last seen him, he and his family had moved to Costa Mesa, not far from the church. Naturally, we were happy to see Glen and eager to renew the friendship. Glen began attending our church and soon afterward he brought his brother, Floyd, and his family. In time, Floyd became one of my closest friends. Floyd and Diane York not only attended the church, they also brought several other families whose enthusiastic response to the ongoing study of the Scriptures encouraged us and opened other doors for ministry.

During the time we lived in Huntington Beach, God was bringing to fulfillment the purposes for which He had been preparing me since infancy. But He was also preparing us for a future work that would be as fantastic as it was farfetched. That is how the will of God unfolds in our lives, how we move forward, and how our progress leads from one season to the next. Everything is preparation for something else. Every story is part of a larger story. Every event, regardless of whether it seems good or bad, is a seed planted, watered, sprouted, or readied for harvest.

Even though the church was healthy and growing, and we had put down roots and developed close friendships through the five years we were in Huntington Beach, when God decided it was time to move us on we obeyed. We had discovered the ways He had made us ready for the wonderful work He wanted to do through us there and believed He would go with us to our next post.

It is possible that if God had allowed us our heart's desire and we had stayed in Huntington Beach, we may never have had our hearts opened to the much greater work He had in store for us. Beneath those surface desires that push and pull at our will, there is the deeper desire to be where He wants us to be, doing what He has equipped us to do. Soon we would again be packing our house and moving to that next dot on God's map for the Smith family.

....

[1] *Handbook of Preaching* by Nathaniel M. Van Cleave, Foursquare Media ICFG, 1943. LIFE Bible College Publisher, 1983 (reprint).

[2] *The Apostle John, His Life and Writings* by W. H. Griffith Thomas, Michigan: Kregel Publications, 1984 (reprint).

[3] *Romans Verse by Verse* by William R. Newell, pp. 245-247, Moody Press, Chicago, Il. 1970 (reprint). See below.

[4] *Halley's Bible Handbook* by Henry H. Halley, p. 814, Michigan: Zondervan Publishing House, 1957 (revised).

[5] Ibid.

Excursus Chapter Six: "A Few Words About Grace" (excerpt)

I. The Nature of Grace

5. Grace is God acting freely, according to His own nature as Love; with no promises or obligations to fulfill; and acting of course, righteously–in view of the cross.

6. Grace, therefore, is *uncaused* in the recipient: its cause lies wholly in the *GIVER*, in *GOD*.

7. Grace, also is *sovereign*. Not having debts to pay, or fulfilled conditions on man's part to wait for, it can act toward whom, and how, it pleases. It can, and does, often, place the worst deservers in the highest favors.

8. Grace cannot act where there is either *desert* or *ability*: Grace does not *help*–it is *absolute*, it *does all*.

9. There being *no cause* in the creature why Grace should be shown, the creature must be brought off from *trying* to *give cause* to God for His Grace.

10. The discovery by the creature that he is truly the object of Divine grace, works the *utmost humility*: for the receiver of grace is brought to know his own absolute unworthiness, and his complete inability to attain worthiness: yet he finds himself blessed–*on another principle, outside of himself!*

11. Therefore, *flesh has no place* in the plan of Grace. This is *the great reason why Grace is hated* by the proud natural mind of man. But for this very reason, the true believer rejoices! For he knows that "in him, that is, in his flesh, is no good thing;" and yet he finds God glad to bless him, just as he is!

II. The Place of Man under Grace

1. He has been accepted in Christ, who *is* his standing!

2. He is not "on probation."

3. As to his life past, it *does not exist* before God: he *died* at the Cross, and *Christ is his life.*

4. Grace, once bestowed, is *not withdrawn*: for God knew all the human exigencies beforehand: His action was independent of them, not dependent upon them.

5. The failure of devotion does not cause the withdrawal of bestowed grace (as it would under law). For example: the man in 1 Corinthians 5:1-5; and also those in 11:30-32, who did not "judge" themselves, and so were "judged by the Lord–that they might *not* be condemned with the world!"

III. The Proper Attitude of Man under Grace

1. To *believe*, and to consent to be loved *while unworthy*, is the great secret.

2. To refuse to make "resolutions" and "vows;" for that is to trust in the flesh.

3. To expect to be blessed, though realizing more and more lack of worth.

4. To testify of God's goodness, at all times.

5. To be certain of God's future favor; yet to be ever more tender in conscience toward Him.

6. To rely on God's chastening hand as a mark of His kindness.

7. A man under grace, if like Paul, has no burdens regarding himself; but many about others.

IV. Things Which Gracious Souls Discover

1. To "hope to be better" is to fail to see yourself *in Christ only*.

2. To be *disappointed* with yourself is to have *believed* in yourself.

3. To be *discouraged is unbelief* to God's purpose and plan of blessing for you.

4. To be *proud* is to be *blind!* For we have no standing before God in *ourselves*.

5. The lack of Divine blessing, therefore, comes from *unbelief*, and not from *failure of devotion*.

6. Real *devotion* to God arises, not from *man's will* to show it; but from the discovery that blessing *has been received* from God while we were yet *unworthy*.

7. To preach devotion first, and blessing second, is to reverse God's order and preach *law, not grace*. The Law made man's blessing depend on devotion; Grace *confers undeserved, unconditional* blessing: our devotion may follow, but does not always do so—in proper measure.

Chuck's mom, Maude

Chuck's dad, Charles

Chuck's parents,
Charles and Maude Smith, 1950

Virginia, shortly after she
was healed

Chuck on horseback at age 5

Chuck at age 6

Paul (6), Chuck (8)

Chuck pushing Bill in an innertube

First grade school picture
(third row, third from left)

Chuck's tennis team (front row, second from left)

Chuck at age 10

Chuck's high school senior picture

Chuck preaching at 20

CHALLENGE
TO YOUTH

COME
AND
HEAR

PAUL   CHARLES

THE SMITH BROTHERS

Outstanding Young People's Evangelists from Los Angeles, Calif.

One Week Only, Beginning Sunday, Aug. 17

EVERY EVENING AT 7:00 P. M.
EXCEPT MONDAY AND SATURDAY

First Foursquare Church, 2108 Emmet Street
Omaha, Nebraska

CHAPLAIN C. L. MUSGROVE, Pastor

Everybody Welcome---Come Early

Evangelistic flyer for Chuck and Paul

$ $ SAVE $ $
On Your Light Bill!
TURN THEM OUT
AND
ATTEND SERVICES WITH THE

SMITH BROTHERS
FROM CALIFORNIA

EACH NIGHT EXCEPT MON. and SAT.

WHEELING FOURSQUARE CHURCH
4200 JACOB ST.

$ $ $ $ $ $ $ $

Smith Brothers outreach flyer

Kay, before she met Chuck

Chuck and Kay

Chuck and Kay on their honeymoon, 1948

Chuck diving at Bass Lake on his honeymoon

Kay's sister, "EC"

Chuck, Kay, and Janette
in Tuscon, Arizona, 1949

Chuck's brother Bill holding Janette

Chuck, Kay, Janette, Chuck jr., Jeffrey and Cheryl

Los Serranos Community Church, 1960-1963

Chuck preaching at Los Serranos, 1962

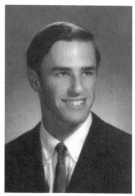

Chuck jr., senior picture

Jeff, junior high school picture

Janette and Cheryl, 1966

First Calvary Chapel in Costa Mesa, CA

Calvary Chapel at Greenville and Sunflower before the tent

The tent as seen from Sunflower Street looking toward Fairview Road

The view inside the packed tent

Calvary Chapel Costa Mesa under construction, 1972

Love Song, 1972

Chuck surfing Diamond Head, Hawaii—looking for the big one

Chuck and Kay 25th Anniversary, 1973

Chuck addresses the crowd before a water baptism
at Corona Del Mar, 1975

Water baptism at Corona Del Mar State Beach

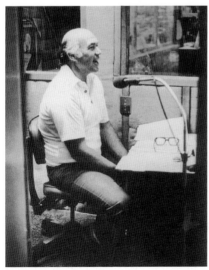
Pastor Chuck recording for the radio

Praying at a Harvest Crusade

Chuck and Kay's 50th Anniversay, 1998

Chuck with the kids during a youth camp at Green Valley

Pastor Chuck at the Calvary Chapel Costa Mesa pulpit, 2009

6

CHAPTER SIX

IF I SHOWED YOU A MAP OF CALIFORNIA, could you immediately put your finger on Los Serranos? Today Los Serranos sits in the community of Chino Hills. In 1960 it was still unincorporated and its sprawling pastures spread over rolling hills that surrounded the small community. Los Serranos Golf and Country Club was popular in its day, but the majority of people who lived in the homes clumped on the hill above the golf course and in the valley below were hardworking, blue-collar families. Many residents were poor, especially those whose homes surrounded the Los Serranos Community Church, Foursquare.

While we were happily serving a growing, thriving church in Huntington Beach, the Foursquare church in Los Serranos had suffered a serious and traumatic calamity. In the aftermath the members were left without a pastor. The crisis was serious enough to threaten the church's very existence, which would have been a tragedy because it had been one of the larger Foursquare churches. So when the leaders in the denomination's headquarters discussed the challenge of replacing the senior pastor, their objective was to heal individuals while recovering and rebuilding the life of the church. The responsibility of making the final decision regarding the choice for the church's pastor was handed to Dr. Van Cleave.

From Dr. Van Cleave's point of view, two signs pointed to me as the successor for the former pastor of the Los Serranos Church. First, statistics collected and recorded indicated our church's growth over three previous years. Secondly, the minister who had served the congregation had been a teaching pastor. Dr. Van Cleave believed that the transition to someone new would be smoother if that person was also a teaching pastor. I cannot be sure I had seen myself as a teaching pastor prior to Dr. Van Cleave's call urging me to consider the move to Los Serranos.

There was no good reason for Kay and me to seriously consider the move. Huntington Beach and the surrounding Orange County area was growing fast. Los Serranos, on the other hand, was not. It was out in the sticks. But I respected Dr. Van Cleave and felt indebted to him, so as a personal favor I agreed to drive out to Los Serranos and take a turn preaching the Sunday services. Other candidates were being considered at the same time, so I felt relatively safe.

Let this serve as a warning to you to give careful thought to the way you place important decisions in God's hands. I knew it would not be right to agree to Dr. Van Cleave's request to candidate for the opening if I had no intention of actually making the move. And so believing that God had graced me with a certain measure of cleverness, I devised a plan that would enable me to surrender to God's will, yet at the same time practically guarantee that the divine answer would be, "No." My plan not only had the mark of genius, but it was *biblical* ... sort of. Didn't Gideon *test* God with a fleece? Since that time it has occurred to me that Gideon must not have really wanted to comply with God's instructions, which was why he presented God with the ridiculous challenge in Judges 6:36-40. This experience gave me a whole new idea of what it means to "fleece God"—or should I say, "pull the wool over His eyes."

"O Lord," I prayed, "if it is Your will that we move to Los Serranos and assume responsibility for the ministry, then when the church's congregation casts their first ballot, let them vote for us, and let it be unanimous. Then we will know this is certainly Your will." Now I had the perfect out. When Dr. Van Cleave would call to ask why we had not taken the struggling church, I could honestly tell him, "Sir, I put the issue before God and His reply was negative."

But when the call came a few days later, it wasn't from Dr. Van Cleave. The voice on the other end of the line belonged to a stranger who identified himself as a representative from the board of directors of the Los Serranos Foursquare Church.

"Yes?" I said.

The caller then informed me that the church congregation had voted, and the vote was unanimous. They would like to invite me to be their pastor.

I was shocked to hear this stranger using the very words I had spoken in prayer. What followed was an uncomfortable pause.

"Reverend Smith?"

"Yes?"

"Well, do you have a response? Will you accept the position?"

What *could* I say? God had beaten me at my own game.

Did you know "humble" is derived from the same Latin word for "humor"? God's humor is often humbling. It brings us to the *humus* (ground or soil) from which we came. When we put our lives in God's hands, we have to move when He tells us, go where He sends us, and stay where He plants us. Nowhere in the contract does it say God will only choose those destinations and activities which seem most desirable to us. On the other hand, if we walk with Him in humility, we will see the humor of His grace that is the promise of a productive life: "some a hundredfold, some sixty, some thirty" (Matthew 13:23). At any rate, we can be sure that we will never outsmart the Almighty. We are only human, after all.

We grieved our move from Huntington Beach—Kay, especially, because she had developed so many meaningful friendships. Our grief was compounded by the fact that the members of our church didn't understand why we chose to move away. It was difficult to explain we didn't know either and that the choice was not ours, but God's. He had chosen to move us on. Leaving Huntington Beach and God's wonderful work was our most difficult goodbye.

Unlike any of our previous experiences moving to a new church, we arrived in Los Serranos with a plan. In our first Sunday morning service, I announced we would be taking a journey through the Bible on Sunday evenings, and begin our survey of the Scriptures the following Sunday. In order to be prepared, everyone should read the first ten chapters of Genesis. Once we began going through the Bible on Sunday evenings, we would read ten chapters a week. When we came to the New Testament, we cut it down to five chapters. I drew my text for the Sunday morning sermon from the chapters we had read the previous week. This gave me the opportunity to treat important topics and texts with greater depth.

The response was enthusiastic and we soon found that the Los Serranos church was as eager to learn God's Word as those in Huntington Beach. The discovery of this unmet need in the Christian community revolutionized my whole concept of ministry. Until this breakthrough, my perspective of the church had been that it was an outpost in a dark world where people came to get saved and be filled with God's Spirit. But now I discovered the spiritual growth that occurred in people was a result of simply reading through the Bible and teaching what God has inspired. Knowledge of biblical truth not only resulted in greater maturity for church members, but the growth of the church as well. People began driving from other communities to attend our church so they could learn the Bible.

This simple strategy of teaching through the Bible constituted a departure from everything I had previously learned in church, Bible college, and practiced in my ministry. Foursquare evangelism is distinct in the way it represents Jesus Christ, but the greater emphasis was always placed on evangelism. At our annual conferences noteworthy speakers such as Oswald J. Smith repeatedly reminded us "the primary purpose of the church is the evangelization of the world." This theme was drilled into my head as a college student and as a young minister so much that when I entered ministry all of my early sermons aimed to inspire people to leave their life of sin, believe in Jesus, be converted, and receive the gift of eternal life.

I can hardly describe the disappointment and frustration of working hours on a sermon with the goal of saving sinners, believing that even the hardest heart couldn't resist the invitation to come to Jesus—and then taking my place in the pulpit, opening my Bible, and looking up only to find that there wasn't a single "sinner" in the building. What does a preacher do when faced with this situation? Most of us laid into the saints for not bringing the sinners. With slight modifications, the theme of the sermon shifted from urging unbelievers to repent to shaming believers with guilt for not doing more to win the lost. Perhaps they are not *truly* committed to Jesus. Certainly God must be disappointed with them.

No good can come from this kind of preaching—or more accurately, haranguing. Church members adopt a defeatist attitude about their relationship with God. They come to church not to be built up— but to be absolved from another week of living a substandard level of Christian commitment. The preacher's authority is the exact opposite of Paul's authority, which he said was "for edification and not for your destruction" (2 Corinthians 10:8; 13:10). Altering my evangelistic sermons did not result in the salvation of sinners. Instead, believers who should have been built up were torn down. If we take Jesus' instructions to Peter as a lesson for all pastors, we will feed His sheep. But I had been beating His sheep.

Through my other "Bible college"—the seminary of hard knocks—I had learned that no matter how hard they are beaten, sick sheep cannot reproduce. Healthy sheep will naturally reproduce. As I helped the people in our church gain a greater understanding of the Bible, they grew in their knowledge of God, in faith, love, and in all the ways that God intends to shape a Christian life through His grace. They, in turn, began to influence other people through the vitality of their life in Jesus Christ. Telling friends and co-workers about Jesus became second nature. Together we discovered that being a witness is not something we *did*, it is what we *became* as God worked His truth into our lives. And as a result, the church cannot help but grow, even if the growth is modest.

*   *   *   *   *

Los Serranos was a good distance from Huntington Beach, but it was not too far a drive from Corona. John Ezell, who had never visited our church in Corona, began to drive to Los Serranos to attend our services. He and Velma also brought two other young couples and their families from Corona, Glen and Betty Hathaway, and Russ and Doris Gozlan—along with her parents, Mr. and Mrs. Kindred. Their friendship, as well as their presence and participation in the ministry, proved to be a great asset to the church and also a wonderful encouragement to Kay and me.

At this point I began to connect some of the dots in my life. The failed ministry in Corona had caused me to lose heart and give up. Nevertheless, we met Mrs. Ezell while living in Corona and through her, John and Velma. Although our friendship had not helped our ministry in Corona, it was now obvious that God intended to put those contacts to use in the Los Serranos Church. How wonderful it was to see fruit beginning to appear out of what had been a season of drought.

In addition to the families sent our direction by John and Velma, the church was blessed with some wonderful people from the local community. Long before we arrived, the core members of the church dedicated themselves to keeping Jesus at the center of their lives. They longed to become students of the Bible and to learn God's will and live it. So when I began my regimen of teaching through the Bible, their response was immediate and enthusiastic.

Living in Los Serranos gave us opportunities to get involved in our community that was not possible in Huntington Beach. We discovered that people in our neighborhood and nearby Chino knew about us before we met them. The community welcomed us warmly and quickly incorporated us into their lives. We soon found that we could not walk around town without bumping into someone we knew.

A few months after we arrived, I decided that joining Toastmasters would help improve my communication skills. Once I got involved, several businessmen encouraged me to join the Lion's Club as well. With each new contact our web of friendships and acquaintances grew. Doors of opportunity opened to us that we would have never seen had we stayed in Huntington Beach.

From our new vantage point, I could see that the line from dot to dot led to an endpoint in Los Serranos. What I could not see, however, was the next dot to which the line would travel a few years later. The relationships we were building in Los Serranos would become critical to one of the most important moves we were to ever make in ministry.

* * * * *

The decade of the 1960s turned out to be a watershed in American church history. In the '40s and '50s, a new religious force came about as young Christian leaders looked for ways to exploit modern technology and to mobilize Christians to promote evangelism. The "evangelicals" arrived and began building outposts around our nation to influence culture, churches and individuals. The Navigators, the Billy Graham Evangelistic Association, *Christianity Today Magazine*, and Fuller Seminary all came into being. Baptist, Pentecostal, and the new evangelical churches—under labels such as "independent," "non-denominational," or "interdenominational"—began to thrive, while at the same time mainline churches experienced a downward slide in attendance.

The Pentecostal movement that grew out of the famous Azusa Street Revival in the early twentieth century was confined mostly to the lower class. This is hardly surprising, since its roots were in the deep South where backwoods preachers had the gumption to believe God still worked miracles and all the gifts of the Holy Spirit are available to the faithful. The lively, spirited music of Pentecostalism derived from African-American churches reconfigured worship to make it their own, like Israel's "songs of Zion" that kept Jerusalem in its heart while in exile.

Pentecostalism continued as a lower-class movement until mid-century. Then suddenly, believers from the opposite end of the social pyramid took an interest in what had been occurring among Pentecostals. Episcopalian leaders like Dennis Bennett and Joan Baker introduced the life of the Spirit to others within their denomination. As Pentecostalism spread into the upper class, it morphed into the charismatic movement—identified with the *charismata* or gifts of the Spirit (1 Corinthians 12:8-10)—rather than the noise and chaos associated with the day of Pentecost (Acts 2:1-4).

In the early period of the charismatic movement, it did not have the endorsement or support of Episcopal, Roman Catholic, or other mainline denominational churches. Most of its rapid growth happened in homes where people met to listen to recorded sermons on the Holy Spirit and spiritual gifts. They then spent time waiting for God to perform signs and wonders. In many instances, the biblical quality of the teaching they received was substandard. Some of these small groups sought out local or visiting Bible teachers to come to their homes and teach, asking them questions and probing deeper into some of the more confusing aspects of the charismatic experience. Several such groups at this time met in Upland and Claremont—rural communities not far from Los Serranos.

Word got around that a pastor in a Pentecostal church in Los Serranos was a Bible teacher. So one day I got a call from Bob Lewis, who introduced himself as a charismatic Episcopalian who wanted to know what the Bible had to say about the Holy Spirit. He told me about a group of believers that met in his home and asked if I would teach the Bible and answer questions. This invitation presented a new and exciting opportunity to move outside the walls of our own denomination and religious culture.

I accepted the invitation. Soon after I began meeting with these wonderful people, I realized their hunger for the Scriptures was even greater than their desire to experience supernatural phenomena. So I led them through in-depth Bible studies through various books. Together we discovered the theological and spiritual richness in Paul's letter to the Ephesians and felt it move us toward the dynamic experience of spiritual community that he describes. Somehow, like believers in many churches across the nation, these people spent many years in the faith without ever reading Ephesians. In fact, they had hardly ever opened their Bibles. But now they were developing a voracious appetite for God's Word.

One opportunity led to another and before long I found myself teaching home Bible studies within a fifty-mile radius two or three times a week. Looking back on the rapid expansion of the ministry during those years, it now seems that alongside the steady growth of the charismatic movement, there was a parallel growth in home Bible studies to what we could refer to as the expository movement. Churches all around California that taught the Bible began to make their mark—from Peninsula Bible Church in Palo Alto where Ray Stedman taught to Grace Community Church in Los Angeles where John MacArthur was the teaching pastor in 1969.

* * * * *

The pastors' conferences hosted by the Foursquare Church had always been one of the highlights of the year for Kay and me. Those conferences provided us with encouragement through the messages of gifted speakers and the opportunity to catch up with our colleagues in other places—even other nations. Our favorite treat, however, was the time we were able to spend with Kay's sister, EC, who had founded the first Foursquare church in Phoenix, Arizona. Together with her best friend, Mary Jane May, EC made the conferences fun and rewarding as well as inspirational.

We had been in Los Serranos for about two years when we received the invitation for the Phoenix Bible Conference. Fortunately for us, we would be able to stay in EC's home and not have to worry about hotel expenses. Our youngest child, Cheryl, was still an infant, so we thought it best to bring her with us. We made all the arrangements and began looking forward to another great experience with family, friends, and colleagues. Everything fell into place so well that I could not possibly have foreseen the disaster waiting for us at the conference—a disaster that was the consequence of two shifting philosophies of church and ministry. I stood on one side of the divide, surveying the alterations God had made in my ministry in the last five years and how that would influence the shape of my ongoing work. On the other side of the divide a significant changing of the guard had occurred in the local leadership of our denomination.

Several months prior to the conference it occurred to me that the Foursquare name was a problem. The Foursquare denomination itself was not a problem, nor did I have any serious conflicts with its leaders or beliefs. I imagined I would serve alongside all of the wonderful people in the Foursquare Church for the rest of my life. My discomfort had to do with the *name*. As our contact with the community outside our church increased, I frequently found myself having to explain what the word "Foursquare" meant. Some people assumed it was some kind of cult, while others would say things like, "You guys are holy rollers, right?"

My idea of God's purpose for the church and ministry had undergone a significant change since my Bible college days. As I re-examined the Scriptures, it became obvious that the church was for the people of God. Ministry is meant to edify the members—and the lives and worship of the members are meant to glorify God. Although the church still has an evangelistic role in this present age, I no longer believed its primary purpose was the evangelization of the world but the "edifying of the saints." It also occurred to me that God proclaimed His gospel through the lives of growing Christians and that more people were drawn to Jesus through these "average members" than any preacher's brilliantly-crafted sermon.

My perspective of ministry was also being altered by the real turn toward grace that had begun while teaching the book of Romans in Huntington Beach. Trying to evoke guilt in people in order to get them more involved in active service to God did not harmonize with grace. A constant diet of guilt is demoralizing, whereas the very nature of grace is inspiring and energizing. So even though I was not interested in trying to make radical changes in Foursquare philosophy or policies, I felt I needed more freedom to follow the trail God had been revealing to me. It had not yet occurred to me to leave my denomination; I merely wanted more freedom within it.

While these concerns brewed in my mind on the way to the conference—that is to say, the Foursquare name, the purpose of the church, and using guilt rather than grace for motivation—an important change had been made in the strategy, objective and content of the conference itself. For several years, Dr. Van Cleave had been responsible for the theme of our conferences. He had chosen the speakers and topics he felt would be of the greatest value for those of us who had dedicated our lives to serving God in local churches. He knew the difficulties and hardships many of us faced. He also understood the importance of spiritual renewal and ongoing education. But Dr. Van Cleave had been replaced by a new superintendent with a radically different agenda.

*   *   *   *   *

With only a few exceptions, Foursquare congregations were small. From a sociological perspective, that's hardly surprising. Pentecostalism had never gone mainstream in the culture of North America. The spiritual gift that was the hallmark of Pentecostalism, "speaking in tongues," was strange enough to modern ears to scare off more people than it drew. The working-class families that found shelter and healing in Pentecostal churches did not usually exercise much influence in their communities. So any Foursquare church that boasted a congregation of one or two hundred was somewhat of a miracle in itself.

But when people are convinced they possess an aspect of God's truth that all other churches are missing—especially if these people believe that God regularly performs astonishing miracles to exalt His people and confound His enemies—they expect their church will be the biggest and the best. After all, tens of thousands packed Angelus Temple in the days when Sister Aimee proclaimed the

Foursquare Gospel. Moreover, if the Pentecostal phenomenon was the outpouring of God's Spirit that signaled we were living in the last days, then we would expect it to sweep the nation like one of the earlier Great Awakenings. Logic would suggest that the churches would grow and advance right up to the return of our Lord Jesus—that is, unless God had withdrawn His Spirit from us. Therefore, a few leaders within the Foursquare denomination considered the small church a problem that needed solving.

One solution was for our churches to create programs and host events that would bring sinners through our doors. It was not at all unusual for regional headquarters to encourage competition between churches. They would set up a contest between churches to determine which one could produce the greatest increase in attendance in a three-month period. When the contest ended, the loser would have to perform some kind of service for the winner. Needless to say, not all of the programs launched by our churches to win these contests reflected biblical ideals. Publicly advertised events ran the gamut from gimmicky to gruesome. One pastor took out an ad in the local paper in which he announced that if his church attendance increased to two hundred people, he would stand on his head on the roof of the church in bright red slacks. I never heard whether he achieved his goal, but I doubt that such a contrivance could have a happy ending.

Prior to my shift to expository teaching, I took the more moderate approach to church growth by laying on our members the burden of bringing the lost sheep in their neighborhoods, schools, and workplaces to church. The underlying assumption was that simply getting someone to church was the easy part. Once they were inside, it was up to the preacher to use his spiritual anointing and skills to talk these people into salvation.

But when we began teaching through the Bible, the Scriptures themselves worked wonderfully to influence our people in the community. They brought people to faith in Jesus because through the teaching of the Word of God they were being "perfected for the work of the ministry" (Ephesians 4:11-16).

* * * * *

Once Dr. Van Cleave was no longer in charge of the annual conference, his vision was instantly discarded. Instead of being designed for spiritual renewal, the conference became aggressively motivational. For the first time, we felt like we were attending a sales convention rather than a Bible conference. The clear message of every meeting was to return home and produce more church members.

Our new superintendent had been a minister in Oregon before being called to become one of the denominational leaders in Southern California. It was announced that in the main session of the conference, the title for his presentation would be, "The 'Secret' of How My Church Won the National Sunday School Contest." In that session, he gave us his philosophy for increasing church attendance, which he named, "Growth by Strategy." In his talk he told us that competition was "a great motivator." He further stated that, "We recognize that competition is a 'carnal' motivation (i.e., behavior that is spiritually or morally corrupt), but it works because the majority of our church members are carnal."

He then gave us the following instructions:

1. Each pastor was to choose and challenge another pastor to a pre-Easter contest.

2. We were to place two large thermometers in the sanctuary, one to illustrate the church's attendance and the other to indicate the attendance of the competing church (the temperature would rise as attendance increased). Every Sunday these thermometers would be visible to the congregation as a reminder to be busy each week inviting people to church.

3. We were to place a telephone on the platform to communicate with the competing church.

4. Each week of the contest, we were to draw the congregation's attention to how they were faring in the competition.

5. We were told that during the Sunday service, the phone would ring. The competing church would inform us of the attendance in their service that morning. If our attendance was higher, we were to remind the people how hard the other church would work in the coming week to pull ahead. Therefore we must work that much harder. If our attendance was lower than the other church, we were to give the people a pep talk to get them really motivated.

6. At the end of the contest, the losing church had to make a purchase to provide something for the winning church.

From the time I had been in Bible college, where students were grouped into rival teams—down to this annual conference—competition had been used to motivate students, pastors, and church members. It had spurred students from the daytime school to defeat students from the nighttime school in Bible quizzes, and now it was promoted as the driving force behind church growth.

As the superintendent finished his presentation, a pastor in the auditorium jumped to his feet and shouted, "This is a tremendous idea! But I move that we expand the competition. Rather than confine the competition to our churches, let's challenge the superintendent of another district and match our district to theirs!" I recognized the pastor who made this motion and immediately discerned that although his outburst was intended to appear spontaneous, it had been planned prior to the general session. Before he sat down, another plant shot up and yelled, "I second the motion!" At that point the superintendent immediately called out, "All in favor, stand to your feet." All over the auditorium, ministers stood to cast their vote for the motion.

During the superintendent's speech, I was holding my daughter, Cheryl, who was sleeping soundly in my arms. The presentation had not felt right to me anyway, so I assumed that holding Cheryl was reason enough to remain seated. God had already been leading me in another direction and I saw no need to join the crowd standing all around me. Besides, the whole thing was obviously contrived and I probably would have felt like a sucker if I had stood.

Some of my friends noticed that I remained in my chair, and perhaps questioning themselves as to why they were standing, they began to sit back down. Before the conference organizers could relish their victory, they noticed our corner of the building where all the ministers were either abstaining or casting a "no" vote. This not only presented a difficulty—they needed the participation of every church in our district—but they took it as a slap in the face. Because they had based their projections and plans for the next quarter on this contest, having carefully planned the conference to elicit unanimous support, they interpreted our non-participation in the vote as insubordination. And before long, it was clear to me that in their minds, I was the ringleader.

As people exited the auditorium after the meeting, the superintendent approached me. Before I could shift my daughter in my arms to shake his hand, he informed me that I was guilty of the "sin of rebellion and witchcraft." He added that by my example, others had been led astray.

Listening to his charges, it suddenly became clear to me why I had not been completely comfortable with his presentation. "Well, to be honest," I began, "when you introduced the idea of a contest, you admitted that it was based on competition, which is a carnal form of motivation. You also claimed that most of our church members are carnal, and that is where you lost my vote. Then, when the two ministers in the audience spoke out, I realized it was a set-up. Since you recognize the appeal of competition to a carnal mind, then you must think that all of us—all the ministers attending this conference—are carnal, because you're using competition to motivate us. I confess that I'm more carnal than I wish to be, but it is my conviction that our job is to turn our people away from their

CHUCK SMITH: A MEMOIR OF GRACE

carnal behavior and inspire them to walk in holiness and the fear of God. If you lead us out of carnality and into sanctification, I'll get behind you one hundred percent. But to appeal to the carnal nature of people in my church goes against my conscience."

The superintendent let me know in no uncertain terms that I had not changed his mind and that unless I got on board, I was living in defiance to God's will. In spite of my misgivings, I had to respect this Christian leader, because other leaders I respected had placed him over my region. When he stepped into the position Dr. Van Cleave had occupied, he became my pastor as Van Cleave had been my pastor. So when we returned to EC's home that evening, I went into our room, got on my knees, and prayed, "Lord, You know my heart. I do not believe that I am rebelling against You. I feel this whole contest and the reasoning behind it is wrong. I am only rebelling against what I feel is wrong. You know it is not my desire to rebel against You."

While I was praying, a verse from the book of Acts suddenly came to mind, "And the Lord added to the church daily such as should be saved" (Acts 2:47). The relevance of this verse to my situation was too obvious to miss. Comforted by God's Word, I said, "Thank You, Lord." It was necessary for me to go to God, search my heart, and lay my actions before Him because I had been accused of a serious sin. Had I been guilty, it would have been necessary for me to repent before God, the superintendent, and all those people who were influenced by my actions. But what I received that night in prayer was a release from God and permission to follow my conscience.

Kay and I returned to Los Serranos and devoted ourselves to the work we had already begun—without the thermometer, the telephone on stage, or the hyped-up competition. Each month, just as we had always done before, we faithfully filed our financial and attendance records with the denominational headquarters. A few months went by and one afternoon we received a wire from the superintendent. "Congratulations!" it read, "Your church has won first place in the regional church attendance contest."

Soon after the wire, a letter arrived from the superintendent informing us that a big rally was being planned for the churches from both districts in which the competition had been held. He wrote, "We have scheduled twenty minutes for you to address the rally and explain how you organized and motivated your people to win the contest." I had to write him back and explain that our church members did not even know about the contest. I did not need twenty minutes to explain that the Lord had added to the church daily such as should be saved.

In the meantime, I had been learning the official protocol for conducting business meetings through the Lion's Club. At that time, almost every board of directors in both for-profit and non-profit organizations followed the procedures set forth in *Robert's Rules of Order*. By the time our next general conference rolled around, I attended the business meeting. When the governing board opened the floor for discussion, I stood and made a motion that each Foursquare church be allowed to change its name if they so desired. The directors, who seemed taken by surprise, voted to "table" that discussion for the next meeting. I accepted their ruling and sat down. But having become familiar with proper protocol, I also knew that their decision would work in my favor.

When they began the next business meeting and were about to address the first item on their agenda, I stood up and interrupted the proceedings. "Sirs," I said, "in our last meeting a motion was made and tabled. According to the correct rules of procedure, that item must be addressed before any other business can be discussed." I repeated the motion to give our pastors the freedom to rename their churches. Someone seconded the motion, it was discussed, and when it came to a vote, the motion failed to pass. However, several years later Foursquare churches adopted the practice of removing the denominational name from their titles.

It was clear to us that "Los Serranos Community Church" was less threatening or confusing than having "Foursquare" somewhere in the name. But in perspective I now realize that the real benefit to me was the discovery of what I might be able to do if I led a non-denominational church without having to drag around the weight of that name. I began to dream of a ministry in which I could hear from God and do as He led without having to conform to the limitations, expectations, and stipulations set by people in a headquarters conference room far removed from where I and the people I served, lived and worked.

7

CHAPTER SEVEN

ON EASTER SUNDAY 1963, MORE PEOPLE crowded into the sanctuary of the Los Serranos Community Church than on any previous weekend. That was the last Sunday we were to be with the wonderful folks in Los Serranos. The following week we were ministering to a new congregation back in Orange County, braced for our next adventure.

In retrospect, we see that those three years in Los Serranos were a formative stage in God's development of our ministry. During that time, we built on the foundation He had laid for our lives in Huntington Beach. Now that we had discovered how desperate believers were to know and understand the Scriptures, we restructured our weekly services to give greater attention to Bible teaching.

In the tradition at Los Serranos, the Sunday routine usually consisted of two separate morning services and one evening meeting. In the morning, we first met for Sunday school and adult Bible class. During this time, families were divided according to grade levels and sent to their respective classes where they followed a curriculum purchased from a well-known Christian publisher. Afterward, we would have a short break before everyone filed into the sanctuary for the morning worship service. The children usually sat in the first couple of rows and were involved in the beginning of the service. Then they would either be ushered out for children's church or they would join their parents for the remainder of the service.

I suppose the theme of Sunday nights could best be described as revival. The roots of Pentecostalism can be found in the holiness movement and tent revival meetings of the nineteenth and early twentieth century. The twofold purpose of revival was the salvation of sinners and to elicit a greater devotion to God from His saints. So on Sunday nights we would preach to save the lost and motivate the found.

This system contained obvious design flaws. For example, some families chose to attend just one of the Sunday morning meetings, even though the explicit purpose was that they attend both. Some parents dropped their children off for Sunday school, but did not attend either meeting themselves. Then there were the difficulties— and distractions—of small children who found it impossible to sit quietly through a sermon intended for an adult audience.

During the 1950s and 60s, businesses began to change their long-standing policy of closing their stores on Sundays. Initially, out of respect for customers who wished to attend church before engaging in commerce, stores that chose to open on Sundays waited until the afternoon. But policies respecting the role of church in American life quickly disappeared. And when Disneyland debuted its first theme park in Anaheim, California in 1955, it did so on a Sunday morning. Before long, believers discovered they simply did not have enough time to spend several hours at church on Sunday. The church lost its monopoly on the national "day of rest." Families suddenly found sporting events, shopping centers, and sources of entertainment competing for their Sunday "free time." They decided they no longer wanted to spend their entire mornings sitting in chairs listening to Bible lessons and sermons.

I decided to make some changes. My goal was not to re-invent church, but simply to re-work our schedule to accommodate my new emphasis on Bible teaching. Rather than holding both the adult Bible class and the worship service on Sunday morning, we moved the class to Sunday evening and dropped the curriculum. Instead, I taught a survey of the whole Bible. We continued to provide Sunday school for the children, but held their classes during the morning worship service. That way they did not need to squirm through a service designed for their parents. With these simple changes, we not only added an hour to everyone's Sunday morning, but we also managed to draw into regular attendance those parents who had formerly dropped their children off for Sunday school and then driven away.

* * * * *

The whole time we were in Los Serranos, my mother drove out for our Sunday services and often spent the weekend with us. Other than her graying hair and a few wrinkles, Mom showed no signs of aging. She was thrilled to see God blessing and expanding our ministry, and was always ready to come alongside anyone in the church who needed prayer or encouragement. Her faith in God was the rock that held her close to Him through all the challenges and hardships of her life.

We were into our third year at Los Serranos when, for the first time I could remember, Mom began to get weak and complain of stomach pains. When her doctor found a tumor in her abdomen, I decided we needed to live closer to her so we could care for her. After a few inquiries, I learned that the Costa Mesa Foursquare Church was without a pastor, so I applied to the regional headquarters and soon received word that I had been given the position. I began driving the family to Costa Mesa on Sundays, but we waited until summer before moving so our three older children would not have to change schools in the middle of the semester.

Once we settled into our home in Costa Mesa, Mom had her operation. Because the ordeal weakened her, we felt it best for Mom to stay with us until she could get back on her feet. Gradually she got better, moved back into her place, and returned to some of her routine activities. In the meantime, we found ourselves busy with unexpected resistance and challenges in our new post.

When I made the move to Costa Mesa, the same superintendent with whom I had the run-in at the Phoenix Bible Conference called to warn me, "Don't change the name of the church!" His warning turned out to be indicative of the sort of problems that arose almost immediately upon my arrival. Not only did I feel like the superintendent was constantly looking over my shoulder, but so were a number of the members in our congregation. Perhaps the best way to describe the tension I felt in Costa Mesa is with Jesus' analogy about pouring new wine into old wineskins (Mark 2:21-22). If God had forced me to stay there, eventually the container would have burst and the wine would have been wasted.

God had taken me on a journey through hard times and remarkable breakthroughs. Along the way, I learned many important lessons about myself as a man of God and about the ministry. God had shown me the importance of teaching His Word and had opened doors of opportunity among diverse communities of Christians outside our own tradition. The church I had previously served had grown to be the largest Foursquare church in our district, and I had left it to assume responsibility for an ailing congregation. I did not come to Costa Mesa with great expectations, but I did assume that having accepted me as their pastor, the congregation would be open to the sort of changes I believed God wanted us to make in the organization of the ministry.

What awaited me, however, was a number of people within the church who were decidedly committed to preserving their heritage and culture. They had joined the Foursquare Church because they wanted to see supernatural evidence of the Holy Spirit's presence and activity in their services—miracles, divine healing, and people speaking in tongues and delivering inspired prophecies. They

CHUCK SMITH: A MEMOIR OF GRACE

wanted a preacher who "got excited about God," paced a platform in mock battles with the devil, and shouted down the power of God.

My teaching method had become expository and my style of delivery was conversational. I had never excelled in the unrestrained exuberance of my predecessors or early mentors who had so deeply moved my soul toward Jesus. Yet I discovered a quiet power in the teaching of Scripture, a gift of prophecy that occurred in the normal course of explaining a text, and the presence of the Spirit working in the hearts of people as they became acquainted with God's Word. To me, this was a revolution. Certain members of the church, however, were not interested in revolution, but in loyalty to their tradition and the Foursquare way of doing things.

In all fairness to them, they had a right to keep the church on the same tracks it had always run. It was their church and I was a newcomer. They were happy with the way they worshiped and with the spirited preaching that evoked their "Amen!" and "Tell 'em, brother!" responses. Although to me it looked as if they were being held back by their tradition, the truth is that in our struggles with each other, neither of us was wrong. We were simply not a good fit.

God had given me a taste of freedom outside of my denomination. In Los Serranos I discovered what God was prepared to do with my ministry when I was not tied to the name "Foursquare" and some of the trappings that went with it. Until now, I had believed I could bring this freedom back with me into the Foursquare Church and

140

along with it, a renewal to my denomination. But I was mistaken to assume they wanted or needed what I had to offer. I brought them something they had not requested and I failed to serve up what they were used to receiving and desired most.

It was becoming clear that the path God was preparing for me up ahead would lead away from my denomination. For the time being, I settled into the Costa Mesa church because my mother's heart was there. She never forgot that God had rescued her daughter from the grip of death in a Foursquare church and that in that same place her husband and children had given their lives to the Lord. She knew many wonderful people in the denomination and had enjoyed working for Dr. Van Cleave as his personal assistant when he served as the district's superintendent. She believed that God continued today doing everything He did in Scriptures, and that the Foursquare Church defended this position against those who denied God's miraculous works in our time. As long as Mom remained devoted to her Foursquare roots, I felt responsible to stay with her.

Eventually, both my ministry and the church in Costa Mesa had reached a plateau we could not overcome. I suppose we all pass through a season in life where we feel we are wasting time. Even then, God is actively working and there is never a moment when nothing is happening for which we can praise Him. We may feel stuck, but everything is preparation for something else. And in the interim, God's grace sustains us.

*   *   *   *   *

A wonderful couple who joined us in Los Serranos decided to follow us to Costa Mesa. Eno and his wife, Lynn, had been in the entertainment industry, performing in nightclubs. Eno was a gifted pianist and Lynn was blessed with a beautiful voice. Both had experienced a radical conversion to Christianity, and afterward, Lynn determined from that time on she would sing only for God. Discovering that they had a spiritual gift as well as exceptional talent, they began to use their music to minister to others. Truly, their close friendship provided us with ongoing encouragement and support.

Another couple we grew to love was Bill and Nancy Younger. They had no sooner moved into their home in Newport Beach when they opened it for a weekly Bible study. In fact, one of the ironies of our tenure in Costa Mesa was that while the church languished, each of the home Bible studies flourished. Bill and Nancy became the perfect hosts. They were not only very hospitable, they were always prepared to take time with individuals who needed spiritual guidance, prayer, or the love of Jesus.

In addition to our growing network of new friends and associates, we still had close ties with other Foursquare pastors and enjoyed getting together with them to discuss what God was teaching us and doing in our churches. We also continued to meet other people in Foursquare circles that enlightened and inspired us. On occasion we hosted missionaries who had returned to the States for much-needed rest and to raise financial support for their work. We were also in the circuit for itinerant preachers and evangelists passing through Southern California. Our district office informed us when an evangelist was going to be in town and gave us the option to have him speak in our church.

One guest speaker for whom we developed a deep admiration and love was Claude Cooper. A consummate storyteller with a British accent, Reverend Cooper brought the Bible to life in vivid and descriptive language that put us in the garden of Gethsemane with Jesus, in the fishing boat with the disciples on the sea of Galilee, and in a prison cell with Paul as he penned his letter to the church at Philippi.

Reverend Cooper was with us for a week of nightly revival meetings. Although we never witnessed anything like a spiritual renewal of our community through such meetings, they did serve to awaken the congregation and refresh our longing to know God. On one of the evenings Reverend Cooper was preaching, he received what he believed to be a word of prophecy for Kay and me. My position on such things has always been to take them with a grain of salt, to "quench not the Spirit and despise not prophesyings, but to test all things hanging on to that which is good and steering clear of anything that appears evil" (1 Thessalonians 5:19-22). To be honest, I remember both Kay and I felt his words were farfetched at the time.

Reverend Cooper said that God was going to bless our ministry. He prophesied that our work would become known around the world and would attract the attention of Christian leaders such as Billy Graham. I fully understand why the elderly Abraham and Sarah laughed at God's promise that together they would conceive and give birth to a son. Kay and I were flattered but we were also amused. How would a renowned and gifted evangelist like Billy Graham—who counseled Presidents—ever hear of this husband and wife with a small church and a few home Bible studies? We respected Reverend Cooper as a man of God but felt he had delivered his prophecy to the wrong address.

One of the blessings God gave us in Costa Mesa was not spiritual, but mattered greatly to us at the time and played a role in an important move we were to make a year or two later. The home we had rented in Costa Mesa was not large enough to accommodate our growing family. Janette was in high school, Chuck was in junior high with Jeff trailing him by a year, and Cheryl was about to enter kindergarten. Needing more space, Kay and I began looking for a home to purchase. Until now we had lived in rental units or parsonages provided for us by the church.

We chose a general area where we thought we would like to live in which would be a good neighborhood for our children. Of course, our slender budget limited our choices, but having experienced God's faithfulness again and again, we knew He would provide something affordable. Eventually we found an older house in Newport Beach, which needed a few repairs but could possibly fit within our monthly budget. About the time we started negotiating with the realtor, Kay received a letter from her sister, EC. Before Kay's mother passed away, she had created a trust for Kay and EC from a small savings account. EC sent Kay her share of the trust, which was $5,000.00. That became the down payment on our new home on St. James Street, the first home we actually owned.

Within a year of my mother's recovery from her first bout with cancer, she became sick again. This time, she would not recover. Kay and I fixed up a room in our house for Mom, rented a hospital bed, and cared for her through the latter stages of her illness. I thank God every day for my lifetime partner. Through our entire marriage Kay has risen to the pressing challenges of family and ministry, meeting them head-on through hard work and fervent prayer. Apart from my wife's devoted attention to Mom, there is no way she could have been with us in those final days.

Many ministers in the Foursquare Church knew my mother because of her position in the district headquarters. So, occasionally one of the pastors who knew and loved her would come by the house to pray for her. Sometimes two or three men gathered in her room to ask God for her healing. After they left, Mom would often confide to me, "They were praying that God would heal me but I wasn't agreeing with their prayer." Mom had raised her three oldest children and watched them put down roots and raise families of their own. She had also lost her husband and youngest son. So in her mind her work on earth was finished. She was ready to let go of this world and join Dad and Bill in the presence of Jesus Christ, her Lord and Savior.

I found that having Mom in our home during those very difficult days kept me alert the same way a newborn did when sleeping next to our bed. I heard every cough, gasp and groan that came from her room. It was hard to sleep through the night because I awoke at every sound, wondering if she was choking or needed attention, and I frequently went into her room to check on her.

Early one morning I sat on the foot of her bed feeling turmoil at having to watch her suffer, knowing I was totally helpless to do anything to relieve her misery. I looked at her hands, motionless and frail, and my mind immediately ran through my history with those hands. As a kid I held those hands when crossing streets or going for walks. While growing up, I spent a lot of time in the kitchen with her, watching her skilled hands as she would clean, cut and cook vegetables, or mix, roll and shape the perfect pie crust. But most of all I remembered the times when I was sick in bed and she placed her cool hand on my forehead, her voice quiet and calm but intense with the faith of a saint as she prayed that God would heal me.

All at once I was overwhelmed by the enormity of the loss I was experiencing. Listening to Mom's labored breathing and knowing that the life of this wonderful woman was slipping away, I prayed, "O Lord, You know that I'm no hero, but I would greatly appreciate it if, for just one day, You would take this pain and suffering from her body and let me carry it. Please, Father, give her one pain-free day. I can do this, Lord. I can bear her pain for just one day."

Immediately I felt an intense impression of Jesus standing at my side, and in my heart I heard Him say, "That is a rather foolish request. Her sin and suffering were placed on Me. On the cross, I took her pain."

"Thank You, Lord," I said as I dried my eyes. Somehow that fundamental fact of our Christian faith brought me great comfort. At that very moment, with a deep sigh, Mom opened her eyes, looked up at me and said, "Honey, the pain is gone." For the rest of the day Mom slept soundly, waking up to smile and say, "Oh, it's so wonderful to have no pain!"

In one of our last discussions together, my mother shared with me the story of Virginia's miraculous healing, months before my birth. Now after several years in the ministry, this was the first time I had heard about the tearful, dramatic scene there on the floor of that church sanctuary, and about the promise my mother made while clutching Virginia's lifeless body. She told me too about the vow she added on the day of my birth, when she offered me up to the Lord and promised to fulfill her vow through my life. In that precious conversation, I gained a new perspective on my past. I saw more clearly the hand of God working through all the pain and all the struggle to form me into the man He wanted me to be—the man my mother had offered up in faith.

Soon afterward she slipped into a coma. A few days later, my mother left her fragile shell and entered into the eternal joy of the Lord.

*   *   *   *   *

Mom's death marked not only her passing from this life, but also the moment we were released from the traditions, expectations, and constrictions of a denomination that was not the right fit for us. We never had enjoyed the same freedom in Costa Mesa that we'd been given in Huntington Beach and Los Serranos. We had seen the freshness God could bring to a church and we struggled to bring that freshness to Costa Mesa. But the church wasn't interested. Intent on preserving their heritage, the core group wanted only to keep the church in place. Now that Mom had passed and we no longer felt obligated to stay in the Foursquare Church for her sake, we were free to begin looking for an opportunity to pursue the vision God had given us outside our denomination.

During the time we served that church in Costa Mesa, several of our friends from the Los Serranos church had called to let us know how much they missed the biblical teaching they had received from us. One of those friends who lived in Corona, John Ezell, contacted us to ask whether we would be interested in teaching a Bible study in his home. This opportunity was too good to pass up, because we knew and loved the people John and his wife, Velma, represented. They were Christians devoted to spiritual growth and providing ministry to others. We accepted the invitation and began the weekly drive to Corona to teach God's Word.

As we struggled with the church in Costa Mesa, the home Bible study in Corona steadily grew. In fact, the life of the community in John and Velma's home was vibrant and exciting. As we had seen in Huntington Beach, believers were eager to study the Scriptures and as they did, they grew in their knowledge of God and their love for Him and for others. Excited about what God was doing in their lives, they began telling their neighbors and coworkers about the home Bible study. New people showed up every week, some of whom had never been involved in any church. But gradually as they engaged in the study, they found God through His Word and through the lives of His people. Turning to Christ in faith, He changed their lives.

John Ezell and the original crew that had been involved in our ministry in Los Serranos determined that if they had a small fund, they could enhance and expand the ministry that was starting to blossom. So they formed a non-profit corporation, filed the necessary paperwork, and created the Corona Christian Association. This allowed them to make tax-deductible contributions to the fledgling community.

While that was going on, one of the men attending the Bible study thought it would be a good idea to record each week's teaching. So he began bringing his own tape recorder and captured every week's lesson on tape. In those days, reel-to-reel tape recorders were the most accessible recording devices. Christian organizations around the country were beginning to make and distribute sermon tapes, but someone needed to own a tape recorder in order to play them. Few people had access to reel-to-reel players, but those who did would host studies in their homes. In this way, people could gather together and listen to recorded messages of well-known speakers.

The men who formed the leadership team of the Corona Christian Association figured they could share our Bible studies with other Christian groups. But then someone came up with another idea. Right there in Corona was a small Christian radio station with a tower near the freeway that was visible from anywhere in town. Why not look into putting the Bible studies on the air? Within a few weeks the first broadcast of the Corona Christian Association went out. Unfortunately, no one calculated what would happen to the home Bible study after one of its lessons hit the airwaves. At the end of the broadcast, listeners who wished to get more information were encouraged to write, and the address they were given was John's home. The following week there was not enough room to accommodate everyone who showed up. John's neighbors were irate because there was no room to park on the streets around his house.

The time was right for the Corona Christian Association to take its meetings to the next level and start a church. They asked if I would like to help them plant a church in Corona. I was being handed the opportunity to return to a place where, only a little more than a decade earlier, I had failed so miserably. But I would be entering a completely different situation, equipped with a totally different way of doing ministry. Of course, Kay and I prayed but we also recognized that this opportunity was the answer to many prayers.

When I announced my resignation to our district superintendent, he gave me a stern warning about "going independent." It would have been unwise to brush off his concerns, but I could also see that if I stayed, I would always be fighting the institution. If I had continued with that organization from fear of failing outside of it—leaving me without a safety net to fall back on—I would have been trapped for life. My work for God never would have been allowed to grow beyond the dimension of the containers in which it was placed. If I had gone from church to church within the denomination, my teaching ministry would have always been root-bound. In my spirit, I knew I had to step out and take the risk.

As soon as we made our decision to move to Corona, everything began to fall into place. A husband and wife in the Costa Mesa church wanted to buy our home, but they had to wait for their own house to close escrow. So we worked out an agreement to lease our home to them for one year and then sell it to them. This enabled us to purchase a house in Corona, and we were fortunate to find a brand-new home in a new tract that fit our budget. This home was a definite blessing for our family and the children immediately called dibs on their bedrooms.

The Corona Christian Center held its first service in a meeting room belonging to the American Legion Hall. That facility, however, quickly proved to be too small so we moved to the local Women's Club. Everyone was pleased with the growth of the church and it seemed that in time we would be able to build or purchase our own building. Until then, we were satisfied with what God was doing among us and enjoyed the blessing of ministering to the largest congregation we'd ever had.

While the church moved forward, its infrastructure began to form and develop. This was an interesting phenomenon to observe. All of our leaders came from strong church backgrounds and brought with them their own cultural baggage. Although we were a new church, we sometimes found ourselves up against old ideas. But during the early romance stage of this new work, Kay and I found ourselves in the best situation we had ever imagined. Little did we know how short-lived this experience would be. We had not yet landed in the field of service God had chosen for us.

The return to Corona was a critical moment in our lives. We had been in the same denomination for seventeen years, climbed the ladder, and developed a ministry in Los Serranos into one of the largest Foursquare churches in the area. We were leaving the security of the denomination to step into a new and untested ministry where there were no guarantees, no retirement, and no plan B if the church should fail. We could have concluded that one dismal failure in Corona under our belt already was not a good sign, but we had a call from God and knew that He is ever faithful. Corona was our baptism through which we passed from "ministry in the mold of others" to "ministry in which God would form a new mold with our lives." This move carried significant risks, but we left the stable institution of our early ministry and never once looked back.

8

CHAPTER EIGHT

I HAVE BEEN TEACHING THROUGH THE BIBLE for more than fifty years now, and I've found that it becomes more fascinating with each reading. From early on, I was deeply impressed by certain stories, quotations, or metaphors that, years later, continue to linger in my mind. Some passages move me with their profound depths, others thrill me with the generosity of God's promises, and a few inspire me with their beauty. Some, God has used to continually keep me on my toes. One such case is a passage in Jeremiah, where God used this powerful metaphor:

> Moab has been at ease from his youth, and he has settled on his lees, and has not been emptied from vessel to vessel, neither has he gone into captivity; therefore his taste remained in him, and his scent is not changed (Jeremiah 48:11).

Sediment forms on the bottom of a wine container if the wine has not been filtered. Wine that sits too long on its sediment absorbs the bitter taste of the grape skins and whatever else was not filtered out. To keep the wine from turning bitter, all but the dregs is carefully poured into a different vessel. God uses this process as an analogy of the nation of Moab that by living too long in prosperity it had become complacent.

It is possible to become too comfortable in life, especially when it seems like everything is finally going your way. The important changes we willingly make usually result from desperation. Why rock the boat when the water is peaceful? The drive to achieve and maintain a stable state is built into the biology of our bodies. Our minds also prefer the security of being in a place where there are few threats and minimal challenges. Not our spirits, however, because God agitates our spirit until He has us doing His will, whether that means comfort and ease or labor and hardship.

God had planted us in a beautiful new home and blessed our start-up church with rapid growth. Spiritually and physically we could have easily settled for many years. Our first few months in Corona were met with such great blessings that we would have never suspected we were soon to be "emptied from vessel to vessel."

*　*　*　*　*

Because our church met in a rented building, we had to set up the auditorium prior to each service. One Sunday I arrived early to set up for the evening service. While thinking about the success and excitement of our home Bible studies, it had occurred to me that their strength was the intimacy we shared. So I decided to experiment with the arrangement of the chairs in the auditorium to see if we could capture some of the energy of the home studies. Rather than set the chairs in rows facing one direction, I placed them in a circle. Instead of standing up in front to teach, I planned to sit in the circle like everyone else.

I was very pleased with that evening's Bible study. The group was definitely more alive and engaged. One man in particular, who had never before spoken up in church, prayed aloud during an informal prayer time. Judging from the response and comments of others, the new seating arrangement was much better for creating the sort of group dynamics that encouraged involvement.

Almost everyone was enthusiastic about the change. One person, however, was definitely not happy—namely, our song leader. To this day I love and respect this man and his family, and I understand his reaction and the steps he took to prevent any future exercise of creativity with the chairs. The altered seating arrangement made it more difficult for him to communicate with the pianist and the group. People could not see his cues as well as when he stood in front of us all. To his credit, he was indeed a gifted song leader and frequently modified songs and hymns midstream to emphasize some important element in the lyrics or tune. So it really was important that the people and the pianist watched him during the singing, otherwise they might miss his signal and continue singing through his improvisation.

Needless to say, he got very upset over the new seating arrangement. I had inadvertently encroached on his ministry. Had he come to me with his grievance, I am quite certain we could have worked something out to accommodate both of our goals. But he happened to be one of the more influential leaders in the church and chose, instead, to go to the board of directors. There he made a motion that for the sake of the congregation's worship, the configuration of the chairs in our Sunday services would not be changed. The other directors, who had no strong feelings about the seating one way or the other, passed his motion. From that point on, the chairs would remain in straight rows facing the front.

As soon as I learned of the board's decision, I knew our time in Corona had come to an end. Until that moment, it had been a wonderful ride. Kay and I had discovered the freedom of working outside the constraints of a denomination and follow God wherever and however He chose to lead. As a result, we succeeded in the same city where we had previously failed. Our first experience of running a church in Corona drove us out of the ministry. In this second experience, we were introduced to a whole new way of doing ministry. Nevertheless, I could not continue there, knowing that simple changes could be blocked by the whim of one of our leaders. This was especially troubling in light of the fact that the change proved to have positive spiritual effects.

I knew it was time to move. But to where? And after less than a year in Corona, how could I justify another move to Kay and the kids?

*　*　*　*　*

Once again I have to marvel at the way God adds pieces to the puzzle of our lives, so that an event during one important phase becomes a critical factor later on. In previous chapters I tracked my friendship with Glen York, how we met at camp, got better acquainted in Tucson, and then landed back in Orange County. As I pointed out, Glen introduced me to his brother, Floyd, who along with his wife and son grew very close to our family. God was about to add another piece to the "York" corner of the puzzle.

Floyd York called out of the blue one day to tell me he was building a hotel in Idyllwild, a small community in the San Jacinto Mountains. He knew we could always use some extra income and asked if I would like to drive up the mountain a few days during the week to help him with the construction. I figured the drive was going to be about an hour-and-a-half and that pounding nails would be a good break from my regular ministerial obligations. So I agreed and began working with him, frequently taking my sons with me to explore the woods while Floyd and I set stakes, poured concrete, framed walls, and built a hotel.

When not in the mountains, Floyd and his wife, Diane, still lived in Costa Mesa attending a small church on the corner of Walnut and Church Street. Their pastor, Reverend Nelson, had not intended to start a church, but one thing led to another and he found himself in charge of a small congregation. Initially, Reverend Nelson and his wife went to a mobile home park on Sunday mornings to provide a weekly service for a few elderly women who had difficulty getting out to attend church. Gradually, several young couples joined Reverend Nelson each week to help set up for the service and run the meeting. At first the mobile home park allowed them to use the clubhouse, but when that option ended, they began looking for another suitable location. They learned that the little chapel on Church Street was available. Fortunately, it was close enough to the park to easily provide transportation for those elderly residents.

We learned later from several people who were involved in the Costa Mesa church at that time about two prophecies that were given prior to my arrival. In one, a man who had been walking with the Lord only a few weeks stood up and said that he saw the ocean emptied of water and filled with people. He said that God was about to fill Calvary Chapel to overflowing, and that the walls of the church would not be able to contain everyone.

In another prophecy, twelve people were gathered for a prayer meeting when one person stood and prophesied that God would lay it on Chuck Smith's heart to come and pastor the church— and when he came, he would immediately remodel the church. After that the church would eventually have to move to a location overlooking the bay to accommodate all the people. And one day we would have a national radio program, and Calvary Chapel would become known around the world.

Naturally, in a church as small as theirs, the people questioned the likelihood of the prophecies coming to fruition, just as we had wondered about Claude Cooper's word of prophecy that we would have a ministry known worldwide. Such things seemed ridiculously grandiose compared to their humble vision for their church.

During the time Floyd and I worked together in Idyllwild, he told me his pastor had taken a leave of absence in order to earn a living. As it turned out, he did well in his new career and eventually both he and the church realized he would not be able to continue his pastoral service. They would have to look for a new pastor. When their board of directors began discussing their pastoral search, the former pastor suggested they look for a Bible teacher.

One of the candidates they considered for the pastoral position was my brother, Paul. I learned later that he had made a favorable impression, but was uncertain that he was ready to leave the church in Victorville where he had served for many years. Someone told the board that Paul had a brother who was also a Bible teacher, and that was when my name came up. So when I received the invitation to come and speak in their church, I already knew something about them through Floyd and they knew something about me.

*   *   *   *   *

I am not certain why the Costa Mesa church appealed to me or why I felt excited at the prospect of serving there. The church attendance was still very small—about one tenth of the Corona church. In fact, its membership consisted mostly of one extended family. But it was independent and the young couples that had committed themselves to its future were active, energetic, and eager to grow in their knowledge of God. I felt an instant rapport with the members and leaders the first time I preached there and when I met with them afterward.

When I told Kay that I had been asked to speak at the Costa Mesa church and they were considering me for the open position, she could hardly believe I was serious. The kids thought I was crazy and did not want to even hear about it. Everything was going so well for us in Corona, why consider leaving? We had a new home in a great neighborhood, we had made a lot of new friends, and the church—which was still only in its first year—was doing well. I had to admit that taking over a smaller church and all the uncertainty entailed in such a move did not make a lot of sense.

But the more I interacted with the people from Costa Mesa, the greater my confidence grew that it was God's will to accept the position. Their church board had to haggle whether they could afford to pay me $125 a week or the $150 I had suggested as a counter-offer, but they finally settled on $135. Even though the move would mean significant personal losses for Kay, she came to my side and let me know I had her full support in whatever direction God led. She hadn't felt that way initially, but after spending a few days in prayer, she told me that God had spoken to her. "I understand," she said, "that His will comes before every other consideration." With Kay in my corner, I submitted my resignation to Corona Christian Center and accepted the new position. In December of 1965 I became the senior pastor of Calvary Chapel of Costa Mesa.

We were warmly received the first Sunday that I spoke as Calvary Chapel's new pastor. After the morning services, three or four families who usually went out to lunch together at a local restaurant invited us to join them. Over lunch I casually mentioned that the sanctuary could use some renovation. The church was not rundown, but the inside had a dingy appearance. As soon as I mentioned renovation, everyone at the table got excited and asked me what sort of ideas I had in mind. On a paper napkin I began to draw a design of the stage and interior that I thought would be an attractive remodel of our worship space. Immediately, the others began making suggestions and volunteering to help. One man said he could do the electrical work and pretty soon it seemed like we had all but the materials to make it happen.

This moment at the lunch table was such a contrast to what I had run into when I moved chairs around in Corona that I could almost feel God smiling on us. I was where I was supposed to be. If they were ready to instantly join me in renovating the physical building in which we met to study Scripture, worship and pray, then I knew they would stand with me in whatever spiritual changes God led us to make. And though we did not know it at the time, standing with me would demand a great cost from everyone at the table. Their church was going to be invaded by strange newcomers, their homes would be crammed with people wanting to learn the Bible, and they would devote many hours—sometimes every free minute they would have had for themselves otherwise—to the ministry in the months and years to come.

Of course, there were still many details of our move back to Costa Mesa that had to be worked out. For example, we needed a place to live. I needed a steady income outside the church, and the kids would change schools again—this time, midyear. But for Kay and me, the big issue was already resolved: God wanted us at Calvary Chapel. We were confident that God would walk us through all of the other details.

As it turned out, God kept our home on St. James Street for us. We had leased it to a couple who hoped to buy it, but after the year's lease ended, their previous house had fallen out of escrow and they had not been able to sell it. So they were ready for us to return, get them out of the lease, and we were ready to resume living in a home that was perfect for our family. Even in something as earthly as a concern over where we would live, God had made earlier arrangements in preparation for what was now unfolding.

The church enjoyed two years of peace and quiet in which we saw moderate growth. In 1967, however, something happened that surprised the world and, in our little corner, gave our church an injection of dynamic relevance for a culture that was looking for answers. When attacked by an alliance of Mideast nations committed to destroying the nation of Israel, the outgunned, outmanned, and poorly equipped Israeli defense forces drove back the opposing armies on every border in the famous Six-Day War.

The Bible—and especially the dispensational interpretation of the Scriptures— immediately took on a new relevance. God had again worked miracles for the people of Israel—miracles that were as remarkable as when He parted the Red Sea and led the Israelites into freedom. This ancient nation that everyone naturally associates with the Bible was propelled into headlines and the nightly news.

When current events take a sudden turn that bring them parallel to the Scriptures, people are ready to listen again to what the Bible has to say. I immediately went to my library and the notes in my Scofield Bible to research everything I could find about biblical prophecies relating to Israel in the end times. I began to find one passage after another that connected the daily newspaper with biblical prophecy. Each Sunday I would open my Bible and point to events predicted by God that were being fulfilled in our lifetime.

The people in our church instantly caught my excitement and within a few weeks our little church became too small for the crowds that wanted to join us. I know of at least one officer in the Costa Mesa Police Department and a couple of firefighters who prayed each week that the fire marshal would not show up as we lined our aisle with folding chairs and allowed people to sit or stand wherever they could find an empty space.

I discovered there was significant spiritual value in teaching on the end times. Three particular consequences stood out.

First, believers gain a proper perspective as far as materialism is concerned. When the end of all things and the return of Jesus are right at the door, the obvious question is, "What manner of persons ought you to be in all holy conversation and godliness?" (2 Peter 3:11). When it is obvious that this world is passing away, it is much easier to obey the command that tells us, "Love not the world, neither the things that are in the world" (1 John 2:15).

Secondly, the realization we are living in the last days adds an urgency to the message. When believers discover that our salvation is "nearer than when we believed," they realize the importance of redeeming the time we have left (Romans 13:11-14; Ephesians 5:15-18). We may know the importance of self-disciplined living and of bringing everything to God in prayer, but when we see that "the end of all things is at hand," we are more likely to show greater diligence in actually practicing these things (1 Peter 4:7).

Thirdly, the realization that end-time prophecies are being fulfilled has a purifying effect on our Christian lives. We do not need to know exactly how the end of the world will come, how Jesus will take us to Himself, or what we will be, but we know that "when He shall appear, we shall be like Him; for we shall see Him as He is." When a person has this hope he "purifies himself, even as He is pure" (1 John 3:2-3).

Unfolding world events in the late '60s revealed that we were certainly in an apocalyptic era and our whole nation was aware of it. The society that had been built on rationalism, science and technology had reached a dead end. Its vision of the universe was of a great cosmic machine that had no need and little room for humans. The depersonalization of humanity eventually caused a student revolution that erupted on campuses across the country. Having given up on the plastic society (plastic being the new wonder product that could be molded into any shape, so that a plastic table could look like it was made of real wood), thousands of young people left their homes and opted out of the American dream to roam the streets and seek enlightenment through drugs and Eastern religions.

I certainly cannot take credit for any foreknowledge of my own. I was never clever enough to develop a five-year plan. I simply responded to God's Word and became excited when some of its mysteries began unfolding. But the theme of my preaching was exactly the sort of message for which a lost generation was seeking and had nothing to do with my vision for the church. God, who had all along been preparing His human instrument, threw me into an unexpected and unprecedented awakening of America's youth.

The Jesus Movement was upon us.

9

CHAPTER NINE

JANETTE WAS IN COLLEGE. Chuck jr. was a year from graduating high school. Jeff was a sophomore and Cheryl was in elementary school—when California suddenly became overrun by young people from across the nation. Uprooting themselves from their homes and communities, these kids trekked to California to join the revolution. They heard that communities of enlightened youth were ushering in a new world of peace and love and that the horizon of the new dawn could be seen from the West Coast.

To fully appreciate the challenge that God dropped on Calvary Chapel, we need to venture back in American history to that decade known as "the '60s." No more than two decades had passed since WWII, and the threat of being dragged into a third world war was very real. Russia had emerged from WWII as a major player in European affairs and quickly took control of Eastern Europe, creating the Iron Curtain. But communism could work only if the entire world was brought under its system. This placed Russia into direct conflict with the United States—the avowed liberators of the working class versus the defenders of the free world.

From our vantage point today it is difficult to appreciate how urgently we feared the danger of Russian bombs landing on U.S. soil. Government-sponsored public service announcements instructed Americans in the early 1960s to locate the nearest bomb shelter where—at a sufficient distance—they would be protected from atomic blasts and radiation fallout. As practice for such attacks, schoolchildren were routinely taken through drills in which they ducked underneath their desks.

The greatest scare came with the Cuban Missile Crisis. Cuba had allowed Russia to begin constructing missile-launching sites on their island. President John F. Kennedy resolved the conflict by threatening a full nuclear reprisal against Russia for any missiles launched against any nation in the Western Hemisphere. We were spared that disaster but the rhetoric of war continued to be proclaimed from Moscow and Washington.

The communist threat locked the U.S. in a political and technological Cold War with Russia. In 1961, the U.S.S.R. became the first nation to put a human in space, but by the end of the decade America had become the first nation to land a human on the moon. Americans have always proved to be able competitors.

*   *   *   *   *

Initially, Kay and I observed the youth migration to California with bemused fascination. These odd-looking young people seemed totally alien to American culture, yet they were our nation's sons and daughters. How did they get so far from home? What was the appeal of this alternative lifestyle? It looked to be a sort of mass regression—as if they'd all willingly regressed to frontier days in appearance and to the magical fairy tales in their thinking.

Today's society is so diverse that it is difficult to imagine the effect the youth counterculture had on people in the mainstream, especially older adults who still knew the value of a dollar. We had paid a price for the privileges we enjoyed—our homes, cars, and household appliances. Many remembered the hardships of the Great Depression that put our very survival at stake. But here were these kids, flaunting their rejection of the very things we had worked so hard to earn. Their behavior was unbelievable. Outrageous.

* * * * *

After WWII, almost every major technological industry, from aeronautics to communications and biological research, had classified research departments funded by the government. The lingering influence of life under military conditions resulted in new cultural trends. For the first time, women wore slacks in public, as they had done when the shortage of male labor sent them to work in factories. A masculine corporate image emerged in the neat and clean appearance of business suits and short-cropped hair. Most schools and businesses had strict dress codes which prohibited men from growing sideburns or letting the hair on the back of their heads grow long enough to touch their collars.

In general, the U.S. enjoyed greater prosperity in the post-war years than in the previous half-century. Returning GIs were needed in every sector of the marketplace. With this new affluence, married couples bought suburban homes and started raising families. In 1946, a boom occurred in the number of live births that continued until around 1964 and gave rise to a generation whose size was greater than that of any other in the previous two centuries.

But not everyone prospered. The nation's inner turmoil erupted in race riots that were reported in the nightly news. While some families talked about the good life and lived the American Dream, listening to their favorite music on eight-track cartridges in their cars or hooked up hi-fidelity stereos in their homes, others felt a revolution fomenting in their hearts.

* * * * *

To be honest, when the stream of young people began hitchhiking up and down the Pacific Coast Highway and gathering in large clusters in Huntington Beach and Laguna Beach, I shook my head in confusion and saw them as freaks—as they were commonly referred to in the media. Kay, however, began to experience a growing compassion for them. At first she was concerned for the safety of our children. Then she began to think of these homeless youth who roamed the streets as lost children. The burden in her heart grew daily and through her influence I began to feel it too.

Gradually our fascination turned to compassion and our compassion evoked curiosity. We stopped asking why these young people wanted to act and behave in strange ways. Instead, we began asking, Who are they? What do they believe? What kind of relationships do they have with their parents? How did they get so lost?

* * * * *

In the early '60s, the United States entered the most unpopular war ever waged by our government. Trying to protect all of Southeast Asia from falling to the communists, young men were sent to South Vietnam to defend a political system that few people knew anything about. The longer the conflict dragged on, with mounting casualties and insignificant progress, the more people questioned whether we should be there. Young men protested the war by publicly burning their draft cards. Numerous demonstrations and peace marches were held in city streets and on university campuses.

To patriotic Americans, these rallies looked like pro-communism. In fact, several socialist and Marxist groups during the mid-to-late '60s drew crowds on college campuses and promoted political activism, sometimes inciting riots. But in time, the majority of Americans realized it was wrong to continue the escalation of this unwinnable war.

By the mid-to-late '60s, environmental and ecological issues had hit the mainstream. The youth who were maturing into this ambivalent world enjoyed greater affluence than any other generation in human history. But they also grew up under the threat of their fragile lives being instantly snuffed out in a nuclear holocaust. So if the human race did not blow itself up, it was just as likely to drive itself into extinction by poisoning the planet, exhausting its resources, and overheating its surface.

If young people wondered if there was hope for them in God, they did not receive any encouragement on campus or from the media. In April of 1966, the cover of *Time Magazine* boldly read, "IS GOD DEAD?"[1] In a related article, liberal Protestant theologians announced that indeed He was. The vacuous vision of existential philosophers found a receptive audience among college students.

The world awaiting the baby boomers did not look like one they wished to inhabit. Society functioned with an impersonal and mechanistic efficiency that left little room for the human person. University administrators treated students like cattle while their professors warned them of a coming ecological meltdown, taught them not to trust anyone over thirty—much less the founders of the nation—and represented the world as a postmodern wasteland. The government sent them off to war and corporations exploited their numbers and labor. Three choices faced the youth: fix the world; tear it down and start over; or escape into exotic realms of transcendence through Eastern meditation or drugs.

* * * * *

With our hearts burdened for the young people floating through Orange County and our interest turning to their spiritual welfare, Kay and I began to pay closer attention to the media coverage that surrounded the counterculture. We listened to experts who were interviewed on television, talked to people in local law enforcement, and read what psychologists had to say in various articles. It turned out that our most direct source of insight and information came from our oldest daughter, Janette, whose social world included people who had left home, dropped out, and hit the streets.

Still, this information was not enough to satisfy us. We knew that the heart of this phenomenon within these kids was still hidden from us. At this point we had no thoughts of trying to bring Jesus to the counterculture, but we were certainly willing to pray for the people who were called to that task. Perhaps God would raise up an evangelist to take the gospel to them as He had used David Wilkerson in the streets of New York. As far as we were concerned, we knew our job was to pray—but we needed to know more.

* * * * *

The "drug craze" came overnight. Marijuana suddenly jumped from inner city slums to upscale suburbs. Timothy Leary, who dreamed of "turning on" a generation, carried LSD from the research lab at Harvard to the corner of Haight and Ashbury Streets in San Francisco. Like a plague, LSD and "pot" swept through the baby boom generation.

The first advocates of LSD were not drug-pushers looking to make money exploiting the addiction and misery of others, but people who believed they preached a message of hope. They intended to recover humanity's lost innocence through chemistry. The message they preached was that war, greed, and the exploitation of humans and the planet could end, but only if the whole world would get turned on. Enlightenment to higher levels of consciousness would result in universal love and peace.

Amazingly, not just hundreds or thousands, but tens of thousands of young people responded to this message as it appeared in books, movies, campus speeches—and their favorite form of communication, rock-n-roll. But turning on was only one side of the coin. Dropping out was the other. They had to rebel against the status quo, to make a spectacle of their non-conformity to the social world of the '60s. To the chagrin of their parents, teachers and employers, these youth stopped grooming themselves, let their hair grow—including beards, legs and underarms—and bought their clothing in thrift stores. Rather than try to be presentable to adults, it seemed their intention was to shock and offend.

To the youth counterculture, society—which included every institution whether corporate, government, educational, or religious—looked like one, big, oppressive machine they referred to as "the establishment." Following in the footsteps of the non-conformist, drug-using beatniks—aka "hipsters"—the uprooted and anti-establishment youth of the '60s were dubbed "hippies."

*   *   *   *   *

At least once a week, Kay and I got in the car and drove around to the various beaches and parks where young people hung out. No matter how much time we spent studying them from a distance, we could not figure them out. We could have dismissed their odd behavior as drug-induced, but there was obviously more to them and their culture than getting high. After all, they did not look at all like the many images we had seen in the media of heroin addicts. They opposed violence and advocated peace. They were trying to create a new world for themselves while making it obvious that they rejected our world. We knew so little about those kids. Our lack of information and understanding frustrated us and made us feel ill-equipped. How could we ever penetrate their culture?

One day, while driving near Pacific Coast Highway and Main Street in Huntington Beach, Kay said with clear determination in her voice, "We have to meet a hippie!"

* * * * *

In the late 1950s I read the riveting story of Jim Elliot and his four companions who were attacked and killed while trying to develop a friendship with a tribal people living in a remote area of eastern Ecuador. I remember being electrified by Jim Elliot's journal entry from October 28, 1949, "He is no fool who gives what he cannot keep, to gain that which he cannot lose." The dedication and self-sacrifice of missionaries had always been held before us as a noble calling, and these five men who gave their lives for the gospel's sake really demonstrated that nobility.

From the many missionaries who had passed through our home, we had learned the importance of having a liaison, usually referred to as an "informant." The informant is a member of the community that the missionaries hope to enter. From the informant, the missionary learns the language, customs, beliefs, village life, social structure, role of families, and the important leaders in the community.

Maybe it was our meeting with the missionaries and the things they taught us that brought Kay to that conclusion. But she was right. If we wanted to understand the ideas, values and customs of this strange new tribe, we needed an informant.

* * * * *

While working full time and taking courses at a nearby state college, our daughter, Janette, met a young man who was a student at Southern California Christian College, now known as Vanguard University. One evening, while she was still preparing to go out with him, John arrived early. I invited him in and we sat down in the living room to chat. John had experimented with marijuana before he turned his life over to God and he had answers to a lot of the questions Kay and I had been asking.

At some point in our conversation, Kay said to him, "John, if the opportunity ever arises, could you introduce us to a hippie?"

"Sure," John replied.

Within a couple of weeks, John was driving down Fairview Street in Costa Mesa when he spotted a hippie hitchhiking and noticed that he was also carrying a Bible. John pulled to the side of the road, picked him up and said, "There's someone I would like you to meet." John then drove to our home and introduced us to Lonnie Frisbee. When we first met, Lonnie's thick hair fell to his shoulders. He wore a loose linen shirt with wide sleeves and jeans with stitching along the sides and bells sown into the hem of his cuffs. Although a thick beard covered most of his face, you couldn't miss Lonnie's penetrating eyes.

Lonnie grew up in Orange County but migrated to San Francisco to be closer to the spiritual center of the hippie movement. It had become home to every imaginable mix of religions and holistic health philosophies, including Satanism. After slumming around Haight-Ashbury for a while, Lonnie encountered other hippies who, like himself, were turning to the Bible and Jesus Christ in search of enlightenment. Lonnie soon found himself living in a commune called The House of Acts in Novato, California a few miles north of San Francisco. Lonnie had returned to Costa Mesa to visit his family when John saw him hitchhiking.

Lonnie was the perfect informant. We sat in our living room for several hours as he answered our questions and explained the religious and political philosophy of the hippie culture. But what we found truly fascinating was the depth of Lonnie's spiritual perception and insight. He constantly quoted Scripture and told us stories of what he had seen the Holy Spirit do in the lives of others. With his long hair, beard, and Bohemian clothes, it seemed he could have easily stepped out of the pages of the Bible.

Kay and I were really taken with Lonnie. He had a charismatic presence that came across as gentle and kind, yet firm. The way he talked about Jesus was like he had just come from a meeting with Him—not the way some believers tend to trap Jesus in history or doctrinal concepts. Lonnie was a student of the Gospels and he lived in the same spiritual environment where demons plagued humans and angels came to their assistance.

We wanted everyone in our church to meet Lonnie. We believed that he could not only help us understand the hippies and their culture, but that his life and message could speak the truth of Jesus to them in ways we never could. Lonnie immediately accepted our invitation, but before he would visit our church he wanted to return to Novato to get his wife, Connie, so that she could be with him when they brought their testimonies to our "establishment" church.

At that time, many Christians had written off the hippies. The message most preached to the counterculture was, "If you want to come to our church and worship our God then you have to look like us." This attitude was understandable. If a particular style of clothing stood for rebellion, irreverence and rejection of social norms, then churches wanted to avoid giving any sort of endorsement to that style. But I think it would be more accurate to say that churches were not interested in having those "dirty hippies" at their services, creating a distraction with the spectacle of their appearance and making church members feel nervous or uncomfortable.

Before introducing Lonnie and Connie to our church, we encouraged everyone to avoid fixating on their appearance but to listen to what they had to say. There were perhaps a few raised eyebrows, but when Lonnie told his testimony, most everyone immediately opened their hearts to him as we had. But then, Lonnie and Connie were easy to warm up to—not only because they were so open and accessible, but because they loved God, were followers of Jesus, knew the Scriptures, and, having walked outside the materialist culture in which most of us lived, they were less worldly than the average Christian. The real challenge would come later.

Lonnie and Connie stayed with us for a week or two before returning to San Francisco. For a while they continued to drift up and down the coast visiting friends, sharing their faith with other hippies and strengthening new believers in Christ. But they had left a mark on our lives and the folks in our church. Through their expression of genuine biblical faith in the language of their counterculture, we learned a new vocabulary for presenting the timeless truths of the gospel with words that made sense to hippies.

Though the encouragement to get "turned on" to Jesus sounded to older ears as though it trivialized conversion, hippies heard in those words a message of hope that was not rooted in LSD, but in Jesus Christ our Lord. The peace and love they craved is found in God alone, and meeting Him is a "mind-blowing" experience. Unfortunately, people did not know God because they were "hung up" in sin and needed to "get straight" by turning their lives over to Him. For many hippies, the crucial moment of insight came when they "flashed" on Jesus' suffering on the cross and became enlightened to the magnitude of His love for them.

Through Lonnie and Connie's testimonies, Calvary Chapel discovered the potential for bringing the message of Jesus to hippies—and hippies to Jesus. As a result, church members felt encouraged to engage in more conversations with young people in their neighborhoods, at work or even on the street. One of the families in our church invited a young disheveled hippie to a home Bible study. When the others saw his wild red hair and his beard, which spread out in all directions, there was a moment of discomfort. But as soon as John Higgins opened his mouth we realized his faith was as genuine as ours. As for John, from that first night the teaching of God's Word captivated him and he began attending every week.

John was another hippie who had come to faith in Jesus and had been studying the Bible on his own. Having been raised in the

Roman Catholic Church, John asked a priest what class he could attend to study the Bible. The priest was not able to help him, so when John heard about the home Bible study, he eagerly accepted the invitation to attend. The study was exactly what he had been hoping to find. He did clarify to us, however, that he was a Roman Catholic and that he would never give up his church.

The more John attended Bible studies, the more excited he got about the Scriptures and shared with others what he was learning. John's conversations were filled with that sort of enthusiasm that moved other people to want the same spiritual experience. The house where the Bible study was held soon filled up with hippies, who sat on the stairs and crammed into every available floor space. So many people attended the study that the neighbors began complaining about all the cars parked on their street.

John spent so much of his time introducing other hippies to Jesus that he hardly had time to do anything else. Every day he was in parks, at the beach, and on the street telling others what they were looking for was available to them in Jesus Christ—not in drugs and their alternative lifestyle. He brought his new converts to the home Bible study and later began bringing them to church on Sunday mornings. It soon became apparent that John and his wife needed a center from which to move out into the community where he could continue his seven-days-a-week, around-the-clock ministry.

A woman in our church had been observing the influx of hippies and the devotion they demonstrated for their newfound faith. She offered to rent a house for John so that he would have a place to conduct his ministry. Soon the House of Miracles on Nineteenth Street in Costa Mesa became a hub of activity. Through daily street evangelism and nightly Bible studies, more and more hippies came to faith every day. Sometimes as many as thirty people slept in the house at one time. But after a week of staying there, John would inform the guests that their training was complete and they needed to move out and carry on the ministry somewhere else.

About that time, Lonnie and Connie returned to Costa Mesa and immediately jumped into the work with John. When the number of people and the amount of activity going on became too much for that small home to bear, a realtor in the church came forward with a solution. He had purchased the Blue Top Motel on Newport Boulevard with the intention of tearing it down and rebuilding on the property. Until then, he said, the hippies were welcome to live there and continue their ministry from that location. Lonnie and Connie moved in and became the spiritual leaders of the commune that quickly formed there.

*   *   *   *   *

When the first wave of hippies arrived in San Francisco, people were giving away marijuana and LSD. In time, organized crime moved in and cornered the market, so that drugs not only cost money, but users were pressured to move on to cocaine and heroin. The flower children began to fade and were replaced by a culture of violence.

By the end of 1969 the optimism that characterized the early hippie movement was gone. Enough young people had either died from overdoses or permanently damaged their brains through hallucinogens that no one continued to pretend drug use was about peace and love. It was just about getting high. The curtain came down on the hippie culture in December 1969 when a young man was stabbed to death at a free concert in Altamont, California. Within two years of that event, three of the counterculture's most popular rock stars had died from overdoses.

Thousands of young people who had given up everything and dropped out of society now found themselves stranded in a cultural wilderness. They did not want to turn their backs on the values they had embraced—non-materialist lifestyles, the importance of the human person, treating all people with love, and the earth with kindness, and so on—but they could no longer find support for their values in the naive belief that all they had to do was get the entire world to "turn on." They needed to find an entry point back into society that allowed them to bring their dreams for a better world with them.

Rarely has there been a time in history when a culture has reached a critical mass in which it was so perfectly prepared to discover the person and teaching of Jesus Christ. The Christian church, which from its founding was an outpost on the margin of society, provided the ideal environment for hippies to be reconciled to God and re-enter mainstream culture, yet without letting go of their belief that peace and love should prevail in the world. Once they heard the message and found a church whose doors were open to them, they came flooding in by the hundreds and thousands.

* * * * *

The groundswell of conversions to Christ was affecting the church as we struggled to accommodate all of the new people in attendance each week. The number of hippies turning to Jesus rose at an exponential rate. We had looked into purchasing property in downtown Costa Mesa but the city council blocked it. Then we heard of a Lutheran church double the size of ours that was preparing to move out of its building. We negotiated to lease their property when they moved and put our small church on the market. But when the time came to begin our lease, the new Lutheran church was not ready for occupancy and our church was sold.

The other church graciously allowed us to use their facility on Sunday afternoons. Several leaders at Calvary Chapel figured that being forced to hold afternoon services on Sundays would solve our growth problems and predicted a decline in attendance. But just the opposite happened. We soon realized that the Lutheran church was not going to work for us because we continued to fill it to overflowing.

We were receiving the inrush of human lives that God was pleased to gather into His kingdom. All we had to do was open our doors and let them come in, accept them in Christ's love, and care for them through God's grace. This is not to say that admitting the hippies into our sanctuary and spiritual community did not present a considerable challenge. A number of churches in our area criticized us sharply with observations such as, "If God has truly cleaned them up on the inside then they would show it on the outside." Even among our own members there were misgivings and doubts at times. But we came to see that the biggest challenges were social and not spiritual. So, constrained by the love of Jesus, we embraced them as our prodigal sons and daughters returning home from the far country.

Meanwhile, more and more hippies were converting to Christ and communal houses sprang up all over Orange and Riverside counties.

*   *   *   *   *

One of the members of our church found an abandoned schoolhouse located on the border of Costa Mesa and Santa Ana. After a few inquiries, we put a bid on the building and won. We knew it would be a stretch for the church, because at the time we did not have the capital to undertake a building project. But we needed space to accommodate all the people God was bringing to us, so we decided to move forward.

For the first time in ministry, I had the opportunity to design a church building from the ground up. I had three primary concerns as we discussed plans with our architect. First, we wanted this facility to meet the demand for adequate space for our growing congregation. Secondly, the building had to be simple in design and construction. It was imperative that we spend as little as possible on materials and labor. As it turned out, the majority of the labor was provided by hippies who volunteered their time. Thirdly, I wanted the church to open out on the beauty of living things. So we designed the sidewalls of the sanctuary to be mostly glass and put planters outside filled with flowers, trees, and shrubs.

The first Sunday we met in the new building, we ran out of room. Fortunately, hippies had no problem sitting on the floor in the front of the sanctuary, including the steps leading up to the platform. We decided that if we held two Sunday morning services there would be room for everyone. But the more room we created, the more people showed up. Now we were seeing not just the hippies flowing into the church, but their parents and probation officers as well. They wanted to find out what had happened to these young people to make such a sudden and positive change in their lives. Word got out about "the hippie church" and people started coming just to see what all the fuss was about. Most of those who came to check out the church ended up staying.

We decided to add a third Sunday morning service, but still we did not have enough seating for everyone. Without too much difficulty, we were able to expand our building by removing the glass walls and setting them back a few feet on each side. But even then we ran out of room in all three services.

Meanwhile, we moved most of our home Bible studies into the church, which meant that we had service almost every night of the week. Hippies continued to have their own Bible studies in each of the communes, which were also becoming more structured, almost like small Bible colleges. In addition to Sunday mornings, I continued going through the Bible on Sunday evenings, taught a midweek Bible study on Wednesday evenings, and started a Bible study on Monday nights for the hippies. I taught mostly on biblical prophecy, because that touched on subjects that were already on their minds. Lonnie also led a meeting on Wednesday nights, which was mostly for evangelism and ministry in the Holy Spirit. Many times I was ministering side by side with Lonnie, John Higgins, Randy Morich, Ken Gulliksen, or one of the other young men who had found themselves in leadership and teaching roles.

During this time, one of our members who worked in the electronic industry asked if he could record the teachings and make them available to other Christians. By the early '70s, cassette tapes had replaced most reel-to-reel tape recorders for home systems and eight-track cartridges for portable music. Before long, dozens of tapes were being purchased and sent out from the church every week. The popularity of the cassette tape ministry was another factor in our continued growth.

One of the truly wonderful innovations of the Jesus Movement was the music. When hippies streamed into the church to worship God, they brought their own music with them. It seemed that every other person could play an acoustic guitar, and many of them began writing songs about their new life in Christ. Almost every Monday night a young person would show up with a guitar and a new song. We spent the first thirty to forty minutes singing choruses and listening to various people introduce their songs. Many of the songs were ballads that described the writer's conversion or some aspect of the Christian life—struggling with temptation, choosing light over darkness, and so on. Eventually we all had our favorite artist that we looked forward to hearing. Some of these people discovered careers in the music industry, using their musical talent to serve God.

Four young men who attended the Wednesday night meetings had formed a band, named *Love Song*, and started writing songs. One night they asked if they could sing, and when they did, the ministry of music at Calvary Chapel took a huge and historic step forward. Until then, what we heard and sang together was folk music—the music of the people. The beauty of folk music was that it was so accessible to everyone. But the music of *Love Song* was soft rock that emphasized the harmony of their voices and considerable talent. When they sang, "Welcome Back" for the first time before an audience, everyone was left in tears. Calvary Chapel entered a new era of music ministry. What folk music was to mass culture, rock-n-roll was to popular culture. The hippies had not only innovated musical worship—bringing to it a style that made it more relevant to them—but they innovated musical evangelism by producing a sound with a strong appeal for the baby boom generation.

Soon there was a proliferation of bands at Calvary Chapel and we began having weekly evangelism concerts. Other churches and Jesus People ministries up and down the West Coast heard about the bands and requested they come and play in their communities. No less than a dozen bands and single artists were touring California, performing their music and presenting the gospel in a variety of different settings.

With so much music being generated in Calvary Chapel, someone suggested we get several of the bands together to make an album. Two hippies who worked in graphic design were discussing an album cover over lunch and one of them, Barry Malone, sketched a simple dove design on a napkin. Later when he tried to reproduce this sketch in his studio he was unable to make it come out as well as the free-form design on the napkin, so they decided to photocopy his sketch and use the original design.

In teaching through biblical prophecy, I had introduced the Aramaic word *maranatha*—a declaration, "The Lord Comes" or a prayer, "Come, Lord." So when the young people talked about cutting an album, they felt it was important to create a record label and name it Maranatha! Music. The first album led to a second, then a third, and eventually became a music company that continued to publish the music of Calvary Chapel for many years.

*　*　*　*　*

Baptizing all of the people who were coming to faith in Jesus proved to be quite a challenge. For several years we had held our baptisms in the harbor at Newport Beach. But when we announced the baptism to our new crowd of hippies, the response was overwhelming. We knew our spot at the harbor was out of the question. So instead, we went to the beach at Corona Del Mar, which had plenty of parking and room for a large crowd. Corona Del Mar Beach has both an area where waves roll onto the shore and a bay side that is protected by a rock jetty. We were soon baptizing hundreds and then thousands of young people every month.

Then the media began showing up. First the local press started reporting on Calvary Chapel and we were frequently mentioned in the *Orange County Register* and the *Los Angeles Times*. Then national magazines ran articles on the Jesus Movement that included Calvary

Chapel. *Look Magazine* included a photograph of one of our beach baptisms that took up two full pages. Magazines from other countries also reported the story of God's work at Calvary Chapel.

Initially, our two acres on the corner of Greenville and Sunflower Streets seemed likely to provide all the room we would ever need. But by 1970 we were eyeing the ten-acre corner lot a block west of our building. We were now in a better position to enter escrow on the property, but we would have to lease or sell our current facility to raise the funds to build again on raw land. Also, because we still relied on volunteer labor for much of the construction, it would take longer to build our new sanctuary than if we had turned the whole thing over to subcontractors. What would we do between the time we had to move out of our chapel and were prepared to move into the new chapel? As it turned out, ten acres gave us plenty of room to lay down a parking lot, cordon off the construction area, and put up a large circus tent as our temporary meeting place.

We were thrilled when the rental company arrived and raised the tent. According to its dimensions and occupancy regulations, we could have 2,200 fixed seats inside the tent. We also laid out a carpet and pad in front of the platform for those who wished to sit on the floor. For the first time in several years we thought we would be able to fit everyone into one service. But that was not to be, for within three weeks of meeting in the tent we had to raise the flaps behind the back row to allow the people sitting outside to feel that they were part of the service. A few weeks later we began to hold two Sunday morning services, and not long after that we added a third.

Looking back at those long months that we met in the tent, I cannot help but feel a pang of nostalgia. The tent certainly presented its share of headaches. It was too warm in the summer, too cold in the winter, and earned us continuous warnings from the fire marshal regarding overcrowding. Then there was the blustery New Year's when the tent collapsed under a strong gust of wind. Fortunately it happened in the middle of the night and no one was in the tent. But God did so many wonderful things in that drafty sanctuary—touched so many people and changed so many lives—that it always warms my heart when I think back on the services we held there. The tent stands in my memory as a symbol of God's grace, for in it I once again took those sheep under my care through an in-depth Bible study in the book of Romans. We all learned lessons of grace that we were able to apply daily in accepting, receiving and loving the hippies who found their way to us.

Looking back over the years, in 1960 I had been on my knees, driven there by my denominational superintendent's accusation that I was "in rebellion." By the end of the decade I stopped counting the number of people we were baptizing. Always faithful to what He has said, God added daily to the church such as should be saved.

....

[1] *IS GOD DEAD?*" TIME Magazine, April 8, 1966, cover story.

10

CHAPTER TEN

I AM NOW LIVING MY LIFE'S FINAL CHAPTER. At this stage of my journey, I appreciate the sense of fulfillment that Paul must have felt when he penned the words, "I have fought a good fight, I have finished my course, I have kept the faith" (2 Timothy 4:7). I could not make this statement apart from the grace of God. It is only by His wisdom, foreknowledge, and goodness that I have come to discover how everything is preparation for something else.

God has His reasons for the pains and pleasures that enter our souls. Through the tragedies we would have preferred to avoid, as well as the good news we welcomed, God prepares us, His servants, for the work He has designed us to do, "For we are His workmanship, created in Christ Jesus unto good works, which God has before ordained that we should walk in them" (Ephesians 2:10). Of course, it helps if you have traveled enough miles to look back and see how an intersection here, a turn-off there, and stopping to repair a flat tire in the middle of nowhere—even when it seemed unimportant or frustrating at the time—were strategic moments in your life.

I have traveled plenty of miles on the highway of life and have come to a vantage point where I can clearly see the remarkable way God anticipated everything He wanted to do in my life and how He prepared me for it. Nothing came too soon or too late, even though there were many times when I would have strongly debated Him about His timing. Now, I see His overriding wisdom.

* * * * *

In the summer of 1971, one of Calvary Chapel's critics wrote an "obituary" for the Jesus Movement which was published in a Christian magazine known for its satire. In his view, the hippie revival lasted only two years and then fizzled. Fortunately, no one told us that the Jesus Movement was over—for the last forty years we have continued to proclaim Jesus to whoever will listen. In fact, when that article came out, Calvary Chapel was in its infancy of all the wonderful things God has done since then. From 1967 to 1972, God was merely gathering and training His laborers because the harvest awaiting us was truly great (Matthew 9:37-38).

Seemingly all at once we began receiving phone calls from churches and small home groups with various requests. Some wanted me or one of our young people to speak in their church. Some asked to schedule a concert with one of the bands, and still others wanted us to plant a Calvary Chapel in their city. There were also those people

who sought to exploit what was happening in our church. Wanting
to draw attention to themselves or their ministries, they asked to
be filmed in front of the crowds. Before we had learned better, we
made a couple of poor decisions regarding people who we thought
had the young people's interests at heart.

As the calls came in, we began sending people out. Soon afterward,
an Episcopal church asked if we could provide someone who
would minister to the youth on Sunday nights in their sanctuary.
The rector was a wonderful man whose heart was fully open to
God and what he saw happening in the Jesus Movement. Lonnie
responded to the invitation and in a short time the church was
filled to capacity with young people.

In 1971 Lonnie decided to leave Calvary Chapel and join a
charismatic organization in Florida. He handed the Sunday night
meetings over to Ken Gulliksen, a local high school teacher and
volunteer pastor. Roughly a year later, Ken passed it off to my son,
Chuck jr., who had been living in Twenty-Nine Palms, California
where he had planted a small church. Chuck jr. taught in Riverside
for about nine months before asking Greg Laurie to take it over.
Within a year Greg had moved the meeting out of the Episcopal
church and started Harvest Christian Fellowship, becoming one of
the largest churches in Riverside County.

At the same time, Mike MacIntosh began taking some of our bands
to San Diego for evangelistic concerts. He was soon teaching a
home Bible study in San Diego that eventually grew into Horizon
Christian Fellowship. Since then, Mike's church has developed
mission ministries in twenty-eight nations around the world and has
founded over one hundred churches or para-church ministries.

Greg's and Mike's stories have already been told in the book, *Harvest*, along with the stories of Steve Mays, Jon Courson, Raul Ries, Jeff Johnson, Skip Heitzig, Bil Gallatin, and Joe Focht.

*   *   *   *   *

In His final days with His apostles, Jesus explained the next phase of their ministry and gave them instructions as to how it would move forward. Their ministry was, in fact, His ongoing ministry through them as they testified to His resurrection—He is alive and He gives life. Jesus informed His disciples that they would soon receive the Holy Spirit and through Him, the dynamic might of God would empower their witness. Then He defined the geographical trajectory of their ministry. Beginning in Jerusalem, they would fan out into "all Judea, and in Samaria, and unto the uttermost part of the earth" (Acts 1:4-8).

The very heart of the Jesus Movement was the belief that Jesus Christ is indeed everything He is revealed to be in the New Testament. His teaching constitutes "the words of eternal life" (John 6:68). His death is the ultimate revelation of God's love for us and the atoning sacrifice through which we are reconciled to the Father (Romans 5:8-10). And through His resurrection we are saved, adopted by God, and given new life in the Holy Spirit (Romans 6:3-4; 8:9-11, 14-16). The reason these core beliefs resulted in a "movement" is due, first of all, to the fact that in Jesus Christ, young people discovered the fulfillment of a spiritual quest they were unable to find in drugs or the philosophies of the counterculture. Secondly, the witness of their spiritual transformation convinced other young people to come to Jesus.

When Jesus explained to the apostles how their ministry would develop, He located the holy city of Jerusalem as the starting point and center of that very first Jesus Movement. The book of Acts reveals how Jerusalem remained the heart of the apostles' work and how even those who went out to other areas frequently returned to reunite with the leadership there. But something different happened when Paul became an apostle "as one born out of due time" (1 Corinthians 15:8). Jerusalem was not the center of Paul's ministry, and even though he conferred with the leaders who were "apostles before [him]," he later confessed that they "added nothing to" his message or ministry other than "the right hands of fellowship" (Galatians 1:17; 2:6-9).

From Acts 13, the Gentile city of Antioch became the center of a new ministry as Paul and Barnabas, and the local community of believers, moved out from there to the uttermost parts of their world. Then in the various cities where Paul planted churches, they became the new center from which yet another phase of ministry branched and spread out into the world. Therefore Paul was able to tell the Thessalonians—who were about as far away from Jerusalem, geographically and culturally, as one could imagine— "For from you the word of the Lord has sounded forth, not only in Macedonia and Achaia, but also in every place. Your faith toward God has gone out, so that we do not need to say anything" (1 Thessalonians 1:8 NKJV). Macedonia was to Thessalonica what Judea was to Jerusalem.

So what we see in the New Testament is that each outpost became a new center. As the apostles and evangelists established churches in the Gentile world, those churches became for those believers what Jerusalem was for Jesus' first disciples. From that new center, a geographical trajectory paralleled the apostles' movement from Jerusalem to all Judea, nearby Samaria, and eventually to the farthest reaches of the world.

Soon after the initial inundation of hippies into Calvary Chapel, we discovered that Costa Mesa was our "Jerusalem." Orange County—actually, all of Southern California—became our "Judea." There are now approximately thirty Calvary Chapel churches within a ten-mile radius of Calvary Chapel of Costa Mesa and dozens of affiliate churches in Los Angeles, Riverside, San Bernardino, and San Diego counties. Other states became our "Samaria," while the uttermost part of the earth is still the uttermost part of the earth.

Back in 1971, a man named Ken Smith traveled down to Costa Mesa to see for himself the ministry to the hippies that he had been hearing and reading about. Ken was deeply moved through his conversations with young people for whom Jesus Christ had become the controlling passion of their lives. When he realized that the transformation in these hippies was real and profound, he came to see me. Ken owned a ranch outside of Eugene, Oregon. He wanted to make it available for hippies who were willing to move up there and use it to further God's work in that part of Oregon.

John Higgins had demonstrated spiritual and organizational leadership skills in the communal houses that he had been operating, and the ongoing challenge he faced was the need for more space. It seemed logical to ask John to move up to Oregon and run a ministry out of the ranch. After seeking God's will through prayer, John agreed to make the move. Within a couple of weeks he and a small contingent of hippie Christians moved to Eugene and founded the Shiloh commune. The environment was ideally suited for Bible study and training for ministry, so pretty soon Shiloh became their "Jerusalem" from where they moved outward, establishing the Jesus Movement's largest network of Christian communes.

This pattern has been repeated over and over again. Calvary Chapel and affiliate churches have founded fifty-one Bible colleges worldwide. All of the larger churches have planted other churches and sent out members into cross-cultural ministry. A first generation of Calvary Chapel pastors—those mentioned in the *Harvest* book—have nurtured a second generation of pastors, who have raised up a third generation. We are now seeing fourth and fifth generations stepping into ministry.

Near the end of the Cold War, but while the Iron Curtain still separated the East from the West, we began to see young people venture into Russia and Eastern European countries. In most of those nations, no formal training for evangelical ministry was allowed. Getting access to those nations in order to hold conferences was extremely difficult, in fact, impossible if their government knew we wanted to host Bible conferences. It was much easier, however, for someone in a place like Hungary, Croatia, or Bulgaria to get a visa for a country like Austria.

Hans and Vivian Sandstrom went from Calvary Chapel of Costa Mesa to Eastern Europe in hopes of leading young people to faith in Christ. Like the disciples on the sea of Galilee, they found that Jesus had quickly filled their nets. They began traveling back and forth between Austria and Eastern Europe, evangelizing the youth and teaching the Bible. In the late 1970s, the Sandstroms invited us to hold a Bible conference in Austria for Christian pastors from Eastern Europe. The conference was so successful that we returned every year, and each time we came back the conferences had grown.

One year the Sandstroms told us about a castle for sale in the resort village of Millstatt. After looking into it, we realized it would make an ideal retreat center and Bible college. Calvary Chapel purchased it and for the remainder of the Iron Curtain era, it was an important hub for Christian ministry into communist-controlled nations.

Through the tireless efforts of George Bryson, Calvary Chapels were planted in Russia almost as soon as the U.S.S.R. dissolved. In the 1990s, our Bible studies were being translated into Russian and broadcast over the state-run radio networks. Although the government has discontinued allowing evangelical Bible studies over their airwaves, the ministry has continued through other electronic and digital means. The ministry of God's Word reaches far beyond the walls of any of the churches in Russia. For example, when my son, Chuck jr., was in Russia to speak at a conference for people who disciple children in orphanages, he was approached by a translator who introduced him to a *babushka* (an older woman) who had a special request. She was unaware that there were Calvary Chapels in Russia, but had heard our Bible studies on the radio and wanted to know if she could get my teaching on the Old Testament on CDs. She was working with orphans in a small village in the region of Kostroma and wanted to study the Old Testament so she could take them through it. We were able to provide her with our studies through the entire Bible on CDs.

There are Calvary Chapel churches in the Philippines, several African nations, Central and South America, Europe, Japan, and Australia. None of this expansion has been engineered or planned, but reflects the labors of many people who have believed God and responded to a need they have seen or a calling they have received. I had never considered launching an international ministry and would not have known where to begin even if the thought had occurred to me. I never recruited anyone for missions work, never outlined a plan for overseas church planting, and never developed a philosophy for international ministry. If I did anything at all to encourage the people who have gone from Calvary Chapel into all the world to preach the gospel, it was this: I never told them, "No, you can't take the gospel to other cultures. You're neither qualified nor funded so it won't work." Otherwise, I cannot take credit for any of these wonderful things that God has done. Even our church in Costa Mesa has grown and thrived by God's grace and not by my cleverness or strategic engineering. I am quite certain that if He had left it in my hands, I would have ruined it long ago.

* * * * *

With our church filling up to capacity every Sunday night—including an overflow area in a separate building with television monitors—we looked for some way to meet the needs of all who wished to join us, without having to construct a larger building. We decided to experiment by taking our Sunday evening Bible study live over the radio and asked KYMS, a local station, if we could have the time slot during which our service ran. We started broadcasting and within a year, the station informed us that more people tuned in to our Bible study than any other program.

The live Sunday evening Bible study was so well received that we decided to begin producing a daily Bible study from previously recorded sermons, naming it *The Word For Today* radio broadcast. In 1978 *The Word For Today* first aired in Orange and Los Angeles counties, and eventually moved to many other stations around the country and around the world. It wasn't so much that we sought to expand the radio ministry—we were simply responding to people who asked if we could air the program in their area. Usually the listening audience of each station where *The Word For Today* was broadcast paid for the cost of the program.

Sometime later, the manager of KYMS let us know that they were switching over to an all-music format. We were given a couple of months' notice so we could make other arrangements to broadcast. After pricing airtime on several L.A. radio stations, most of which were more expensive, we learned of a small station in San Clemente that was for sale. Evaluating the cost factors, it made much more sense to buy the radio station than to purchase airtime from someone else. In 1985, KWVE 107.9 FM began airing Bible teaching twenty-four hours a day.

*　*　*　*　*

Like most people, I have found that it is much easier to feel closer to God in a natural environment like by the ocean or up in the mountains. Innumerable distractions in our congested cities make it difficult to keep our attention on God or remember to be thankful for the wonders of His handiwork. It seems that every new technology separates us from creation by one more layer, and nothing alienates us from creation more than the eerie virtual worlds we enter through our computers.

Ever since I was called to ministry while sitting under a pine tree at Camp Radford, I have believed in the vital role that camping and retreats can play in the spiritual lives of young people. For many years, Calvary Chapel would rent Christian campgrounds in the San Jacinto Mountains and host weeklong camps. For the first few years, we offered family camps in which everyone was welcome. But when our attendance outgrew every available campsite, we began specialized programs just for the adults, or for the teenagers and children. As more ministries developed within the church, each ministry began running its own camping program.

Calvary Chapel now owns several different conference centers and camps. Perhaps it is improper for me to have a favorite, but I cannot help but thoroughly enjoy the youth camp in Running Springs, California. Having spent many summers directing camps for children from eight to eighteen, I had the privilege of designing the youth camp from the ground up. I could take up several pages describing the log cabin architecture we used for every building, the many recreational activities we built into the facility and grounds, and the breathtaking view from the chapel built into a hillside.

But the really important fact is that from the summer of 1994 to the fall of 2008, 334,000 kids have gone through the youth camp. I have been privileged to be present when many of these young people have given their hearts to Christ. I think that of all our many ministries, the work that goes on at the youth camp is among the most gratifying.

*   *   *   *   *

In 1989 Chuck jr.'s church in Capistrano Beach, California rented the Irvine Meadows Amphitheater for their Easter service. They advertised it as "Easter in the Meadows." And when I saw the posters and heard the advertisements, I realized there was a wonderful potential to reawaken Orange County to the truth of God in Jesus Christ by holding a large rally. Having never considered myself an evangelist, it occurred to me that a pastor from one of our other churches would be better suited to address a large crowd.

Greg Laurie's church, Harvest Christian Fellowship, was thriving in Riverside, but he also drove down to Costa Mesa on Monday nights to host evangelistic Bible studies at our church. So I ran my idea past him. I told him I was thinking of renting the Pacific Amphitheater in Costa Mesa for a three-night evangelistic crusade based on the model of the Billy Graham Evangelistic Association. Greg was intrigued but said, "That would take a lot of planning and a lot of work. I suppose we could do it next year."

"Greg," I said, "we're going to hold the crusade this year. We have all the resources on hand and it will be easy to round up the musicians and other participants."

CHAPTER TEN

Looking back on that first Harvest Crusade, I have to admit that we should have definitely put more time and thought into the planning. Each night the amphitheater was filled to capacity. On the third and final night after the seats filled up, the Pacific Amphitheater staff closed the gates, preventing thousands of people from entering. As a result, every street around the theater was jammed for several miles. The Costa Mesa Police Department located across the street from the Pacific Amphitheater was not at all pleased with the success of our event—nor were the people who lived in the surrounding neighborhood.

In subsequent years, we turned to the more spacious Edison Field, now home to the Los Angeles Angels, for the Harvest Crusades. The summer of 2009 will mark twenty years of Harvest Crusade events, and they are as well-attended now as they were at first.

* * * * *

The more I became immersed in ministry, the more it became obvious to me that my education was deficient in many areas. I frequently encountered problems and challenges for which I was not prepared and found myself thinking, "I wish they had taught us something about this in Bible college." Over the years of my ministry, however, I've learned that there are many things you simply can't learn from an instructor. Some things can only be acquired through life experience. The education we receive from following Jesus as His disciples is not exclusively meant to inform us but to transform us. In other words, throughout our lives in Christ we are being trained as well as taught (Hebrews 12:7-13). Like Jesus, we learn both truth and obedience through suffering

(Hebrews 5:8). Godly character is not developed in a classroom or seminar, but in the heat of tribulation (Romans 5:3-5).

God has certainly been more consistent than me in the eight decades that I have walked with Him on this planet. Therefore, everything I have learned and anything I have accomplished is based completely on His mercy and faithfulness. A few of the more important lessons the Lord has drilled into me include the following:

* * * * *

Do not despise "the day of small things" (Zechariah 4:10). Our own hearts are capable of concocting some grandiose visions of how we can serve God or how He should use us. But in His school, God begins with the alphabet. He patiently lays a foundation in our lives before raising the walls and towers. I have found that it is important to be willing to do no more than plant seeds, even if we will not live to see the harvest.

* * * * *

"It is good for a man that he bear the yoke in his youth" (Lamentations 3:27). One of the worst things that can happen to a young minister is to experience early success. It is all too easy for us to believe that, "By the strength of my hand I have done it" (Isaiah 10:13). Until we have sat for a while in failure and come to the end of ourselves, we will neither know nor credit God's grace for whatever good we may do. Nor will we be able to minister grace to others in their time of need and failure. Instead, we will exhort them to pick themselves up and follow our "Five-Step Plan for Success."

* * * * *

Do not look "at the things which are seen, but at the things which are not seen; for the things which are seen are temporal; but the things which are not seen are eternal" (2 Corinthians 4:18). God rarely wastes His time trying to explain to us what He is doing and what it means. Perhaps we should frequently remind ourselves of Jesus' words to Peter prior to washing his feet, "What I do thou knowest not now; but thou shalt know hereafter" (John 13:7). When we stand too close to the painful circumstances of one moment, we lose sight of God's will, and like Peter, are tempted to say, "Never!" (John 13:8). Preoccupation with the troubles of the moment is what makes our hearts and minds vulnerable to panic and anxiety. We need to back away and get the eternal perspective from which it is more clear that "our light affliction, which is but for a moment, works for us a far more exceeding and eternal weight of glory" (2 Corinthians 4:17).

* * * * *

Whatever you do, "grow in grace, and in the knowledge of our Lord and Savior Jesus Christ" (2 Peter 3:18). I cannot overemphasize the importance of the role that grace plays in every aspect of our lives. When it becomes obvious that I have not made as much progress in holiness as God desires, grace fills the distance between where I am and where I should be, and draws me forward. Grace makes what is impossible for me by my own strength, not only possible but also much easier than I could have imagined. It is true that sometimes grace enables us to labor "more abundantly" than others, but it is also sufficient for us when weakness or pain prevents us from doing all that we wish we could be doing (1 Corinthians 15:10; 2 Corinthians 12:9).

* * * * *

Remember the two greatest commandments: "Love the Lord thy God with all thy heart, with all thy soul, with all thy mind, and with all thy strength" and "Love thy neighbor as thyself" (Mark 12:30-31). Hearing the stories of Jesus while we sit in church can warm our hearts with feelings of love, but it is a much different challenge to love the outsider, the sinner, and the enemy. The first time some of the more conservative Christians in our church had to share their pew with a hippie, they found the challenge of loving and accepting others to be very difficult. Fortunately, all they had to do was share a few words to discover this young person was their prodigal son or daughter returning home. We will always be learning that it is not enough to "love in word, neither in tongue" but to activate our love "in deed and in truth" (1 John 3:18).

* * * * *

Prepare yourself—as much as it is humanly possible—to obey Jesus to do something even if it is ridiculous like "Stretch forth thine hand" when your hand is paralyzed (Mark 3:1-5). Even when you have "toiled all night" fishing and caught nothing—let down the net if Jesus tells you to do so (Luke 5:4-7). We sometimes balk at Jesus' strange commands thinking, *But if nothing happens I will look so stupid.* Here is the heart of the matter: It is not about you. It is about the work of Jesus and the glory of God. His thoughts are always higher than ours and His work is always greater than what we ask or think. I may not always get it right the first time, but I have become more consistent in just doing what He says when He tells me, "Open thy mouth wide, and I will fill it" (Psalm 81:10).

*   *   *   *   *

Exercise your best wisdom and always be cautious when dealing with money. I cannot stress strongly enough the importance of handling your finances with integrity. As Paul told Timothy, "They that will be rich fall into temptation and a snare, and into many foolish and hurtful lusts, which drown men in perdition" (1 Timothy 6:9). Quite a few ministers have fallen into trouble, even prison, and "pierced themselves through with many sorrows" mishandling money. In general, if you are "diligent to know the state" of your resources, income, and work, you will always have enough. (Proverbs 27:23-27). Otherwise, greed has caused many intelligent people to act stupidly. When a moneymaking opportunity looks too good to be true, it is. The greatest gain in life comes through "godliness with contentment" (1 Timothy 6:6).

*   *   *   *   *

Beware the praise of the crowd (Luke 6:26). "The fear of man brings a snare," said the wise man (Proverbs 29:25). Even those people who have come to believe in Christ can be silenced from making a profession of faith out of fear of the opinion of others (John 5:44; 12:42-43). When we put our effort into pleasing people, it disables our service to Christ (Galatians 1:10). Sometimes it is good to renew our minds and refresh our spirits with the doxologies we find in the New Testament letters. They always point us in the right direction when it comes to the "glory." "To God only wise, be glory through Jesus Christ for ever" (Romans 16:27).

*   *   *   *   *

I would especially direct this lesson to pastors: "Preach the word; be instant in season, out of season; reprove, rebuke, exhort with all longsuffering and doctrine" (2 Timothy 4:2). In other words, simply teach the Word simply. The greatest service you can provide to the people in your care is to make the Bible accessible to them. Give them the "sincere milk of the Word" in a way that is easily digested. That way they can grow, become skillful in the "word of righteousness," and be able to move on to the "strong meat" of Scripture (1 Peter 2:2; Hebrews 5:12-14). The best Bible teaching is not that which dazzles people with the profound intellect of their teacher, but that which puts its truth squarely in their hands.

* * * * *

For many years I have enjoyed a life of extraordinary blessing and I am convinced that is God's will for every Christian. But before getting to that place in life, I learned many difficult lessons—and I am still learning—for God never allows us to fully make ourselves at home in this world. Had I known when I was a young man just getting started in ministry what I know now, I could have lived with unceasing joy even through the difficult years. But then I knew only what lay within each day's walk, whereas now I see where the journey has taken me.

In the preparation, discouragements and defeats are necessary. Had I been successful early on, I would have taken credit for all that God did. I would not have been able to handle the recognition that God gave me but would have taken credit for the success. God wants to receive the glory for the work He does, so He first prepares the person to be the instrument He desires to use. That preparation includes a lot of failure in order to learn the difference between God's work and your own. God leads you through failure so that when He works you will know for certain you are not responsible for the success. Then God alone receives the credit. God wants to work, but the glory needs to go to God.

I have not been able to tell my story apart from God. This is really His story, for the most important accomplishments of my life have been the result of His grace meeting me each morning as I rise from bed, guiding my steps through the day, and giving me the strength to respond to the opportunities God gives to me.

I am no different in God's sight from anyone else. The blessings He's given me are available to all, and I am convinced that any person can live a life as full and as joyous as mine has been.

Just keep your eyes on the Lord and follow Him as closely as possible. Be patient, for in His time when He finally connects all the dots, you will realize that truly all things work together for good. Even as Paul encouraged us in Galatians 6:9, "Let us not be weary in well doing, for in due season we shall reap, if we faint not."

May the Lord grant you the grace and patience to wait on Him until His full purpose is completed in and through your life, and you have the joy of hearing Him say, "Well done, good and faithful servant."

For more information about additional resources by Pastor Chuck Smith or to be included to our e-mail list for updates by *The Word For Today*, please contact:

THE WORD
FOR TODAY

Toll-Free (800) 272-WORD (9673)
P.O. Box 8000, Costa Mesa, CA 92628
Web site: www.twft.com • E-mail: info@twft.com